THE RELAPSE SOLUTION

Rebuilding A Life Worth Living Sober

STEVE FALLIN

The Relapse Solution: Rebuilding A Life Worth Living Sober

© Copyright 2019 Steve Fallin

Cover and Interior Design by:
Karen R. Power
http://www.KarenPower.com

Cover Images by:
Sergey Nivens

ISBN: 9781793377241

http://www. stevefallin-author.com

Presented to:

_____

From:

_____

Date:

_____

What People Are Saying About *The Relapse Solution*

The Relapse Solution is a much needed approach to total Recovery. It has the instructions to guide someone from merely "Surviving" to a life of "Thriving!"

—**DOUG ABNER**, Appalachian Center For Transformation, City of Hope, Manchester, KY

I would highly recommend this book. I felt great comfort in knowing that there is abundant life after establishing recovery from   trials and tribulations ... whether it be an addiction, trauma or loss. This book gives you a road map of inspiration to connect with a higher power on an awesome journey!

—**DEBRA MURPHY**, CACII, NCACII, MATC, CCS

I found the book to be on point for people in recovery who are not only interested in quitting the addiction but also want a richer, fuller life that only Jesus can offer.   I read it out loud to the members of my ministry and each day we received insights and helpful suggestions.

—**CATHY SWEAT**, CADCII, CARES28, CPS-AD, BCPC, CCLC, Director, Bethesda Recovery

The book you hold in your hands can change the destiny of your life. It is the product of a life serving others navigating life's challenges including staying free from life controlling issues. This book will bless those who read it with tools for living strong and staying encouraged. Steve has for decades responded to the needs of others through education, intervention, prevention and equipping. Steve shares from a wealth of experience and a depth of walking with God that will be sure to help others on life's journey. The information will be practical, easily applicable and life sustaining. Get ready to enjoy the journey of life on a higher level.

—**JERRY STEWART**, Pastor, G.O. Church,

Ball Ground, GA

I really liked the part where Abraham had to leave familiar, past acquaintances and go to a new place. The story about Henry was also very powerful. It showed what could happen if you go back. God gives the promised land, but you must possess it.

—**MICKEY MOSKOVITZ**,

Covenant Community Church, Ellijay, GA

Acknowledgments

THANKS, first of all, to the Holy Spirit for guiding and inspiring these pages. I'm pretty sure my writing would be a pointless waste of time without His help!

I want to say a special thanks to my wife, Ruth Fallin, for being my partner in ministry for over 30 years. You have always been my biggest cheer-leader and fan. Your faithfulness means more to me than words could ever express!

I want to say a special thanks to Lynda Meisen for taking the time to help edit this entire text. Your input and comments were invaluable and working with you on this gave me a renewed appreciation for all the things that school teachers contribute to our lives.

Here's a big Thanks and Shout Out to all the members of the Celebrate Life team at GO Church in Ball Ground, Georgia for your loving and serving hearts. Forming a group and a (trial-run) teaching series with some of this material really helped to make it better. And, many thanks to the ladies of Bethesda Recovery of Waycross, Georgia for taking the time to read and discuss these chapters. Many thanks to Bethesda Executive Director, Cathy Sweat for your help and encouragement.

Thanks to everyone in my family, both natural and spiritual, who have believed in God's transforming work in me all these years. To my brother, Clay, it's been a tough job trying to be a big brother to someone in recovery, but I hope you know that your faith in me to be able to write this book has been a source of tremendous encouragement.

And, to the other (spiritual) big brother in my life, my pastor, Jerry Stewart, thanks for being supportive of my gifts and calling in a way that has challenged me to come up higher. Your consistent teaching has had a tremendous impact upon my ability to express the contents of these pages.

Contents

The Crisis of Addiction and Relapse

ADDICTION... It's a word that evokes a strong reaction in people. Some call it a disease, some call it a disorder, and still others think of it as mainly a side effect or symptom of something deeper happening in a person's mental health. Spiritual leaders and healers will at times refer to addiction as a bondage or the outworking of some form of negative energy. But none of our labels and theories will really solve the problem.

What we think about addiction may tell us a lot about what we believe are the root causes and inner workings; but the labels we use to describe addiction won't be near as important as the solutions we put forth. People are suffering from addiction through all of its influences across families and communities and there's no time for debate. Everyone who can help should help and real solutions may not be as far from us as we might think.

After more than thirty years of working with addicts and their families, I can say with confidence there is no such thing as a one-size-fits-all approach to addiction treatment and recovery. Addicts are as different as people, themselves are different. And, while certain approaches and cognitive therapies may work well to help addicts get clean, the success rate for sustained, long-term recovery is still very poor.

RELAPSE... That's another word that gets a strong reaction. But the causes and failures that precede a relapse are widely debated and, in most cases, we just lay the blame on the addict. It's easier for everyone that way, we tell ourselves, because after all, we gave them the tools, the truth, and taught them the steps that should have made their recovery successful. The problem, however, is that our evaluation of what went wrong just doesn't go deep enough into questions about the relapsed addict's quality of life.

It just doesn't make sense, we say, for someone to work so hard to stop using drugs or alcohol and then go back into that whirlwind that drove them to recovery in the first place. But, the sense that it makes to the addict will always elude us unless we take time to understand how they concluded that the life they KNOW just isn't worth living sober!

Sober but Miserable ... It Doesn't Have To Be Like This

White-collar criminals will tell you that it's not the crime that gets you, it's the cover up! In a similar way, people in recovery often contribute to their own failure because they are so good at pretending, covering up, and

12

convincing people they've got it all together when they don't. This sets up a trap for recovering addicts because they are prone to fantasy thinking and try to go after things they may not be ready to tackle.

The greatest threat from fantasy thinking comes when a recovering addict steps out of treatment believing they are ready to rebuild their devastated life. They may have been told to avoid triggers, go to work, go to counseling, and be sure to go to meetings. Armed with the tools and strategies they've been given, they feel confident, and may tell everyone, "I'm ready."

What usually happens next is far too common and mostly avoidable if we could help recovering addicts with skills for true life-change and rebuilding. If you've ever attended 12-Step meetings, you've probably seen them and you can spot them a mile away. I'm talking about people in recovery who faithfully attend the meetings, work the Steps, and can recite the principles and creeds of recovery like a fluent second language. There are always those who've developed a tremendous head-knowledge but have never had a heart-change.

These are the ones I've come to refer to as the sober-but-miserable crowd who are only a hair's breadth away from a relapse most of the time. They are miserable, NOT because they are bad people or have done anything wrong, but because they have been unable to rebuild a real life for themselves since they got sober.

In fact, recovery has become their life and pretty much the only life they know. Gone are the days when they once had ambition and dreamed of doing great things. Gone are the carefree days of child-like joy they once knew when they were able to be that free-spirit that seems to have gotten them in trouble. What they have left is a tawdry and boring life filled with adulting behaviors they've learned to wear like crutches holding up a cripple.

They are miserable because their lust for adventure has been doused like a wet blanket thrown over a fire. Nothing has been offered that could restore the zest for life they once had. Recovery, itself, may now feel like a trap and they long for something, anything of passion they could do instead..., instead of drugs and alcohol. It wasn't supposed to be like this and it doesn't have to be like this.

Rebuilding a Devastated Life Takes Total Transformation

If you can relate to that description of recovering addicts because at some point that was you or because it describes someone you know, this book is definitely for you. But even if you read this introduction and don't relate to it, read on. If you find that description insulting and perhaps overly critical of twelve step meetings, this book is for you too because it may open up some ideas you've never considered.

This book is also written to professionals, friends, and family members who've experienced the heartbreak of watching a loved one go back to prison or die because of a life of perpetual relapse. I have known that heartache for over 40 years because the first time I experienced a loss to addiction was at fifteen years old with the death of a friend. It was 1975 and we were all doing a lot of drugs. That could have been me.

The twists and turns of my own addiction and recovery are described in different places throughout the chapters of this book. It is my attempt to tell the world what God did for me through a life-rebuilding process that worked. The truths on these pages have kept me clean and sober for over thirty years!

What is written here is not intended to downplay or criticize the great work of the many helpful recovery programs and meetings that help people all over the world. Whether you prefer traditional twelve step meetings or a more Christ-centered approach to getting support, the message here is intended to build upon that foundation.

The point of this book is that there is MORE. The message is that THERE IS LIFE after recovery! But to access that life we will have to make some quality decisions. We will have to go beyond recovery to reach for RESTORATION. It is an attempt to answer a basic question that every recovering addict has, *How do I rebuild my devastated life?*

The chapters are presented as a journey with God where the reader who has suffered from a sordid, addictive love affair with a substance will begin to answer the question, *What will I do instead?*

To those who serve and sacrifice in the work of helping others in recovery, this book is intended to be a challenge to do more. In my own efforts to help others over the past decades I have grown weary of the deaths and loss of beautiful people who looked like they were going to make it. We desperately need to push harder to help people experience a greater transformation that will last.

I am no longer content with participation in support-group meetings week after week with people who are sober-but-miserable, just barely hanging on. Jesus came and shared with us a path to ABUNDANT LIFE. It is not complicated and it works for anyone who will receive it. No one ever said that restoration and transformation would be easy, but it sure does beat trying to live clean, staying the same, and dangling on the edge of relapse every day for the rest of my life!

CHAPTER 1

Traps

If It's Not "Abundant Life," Then What Is It?

Have you ever known someone that came out of a life of trauma, addiction, and destruction? Do you recall meeting people along the way who could talk like they're in recovery and even walk like they're in recovery, but still look like they are miserable? If so, this book is for you and it is especially written for them. It's called *The Relapse Solution* because relapse can happen to anyone at any place along the road to recovery, but that's not all there is to the story.

What if the Bible, in just a few verses, could give us keys for becoming more "bulletproof" with powerful defenses that can protect us from relapse? Is it possible that the answers have been there in God's Word all along for developing a resilient life? What could happen if I truly surrendered to God's "rebuilding" process? If you believe that being "sober" but still "miserable" is an unacceptable condition, then you will want to take this Journey into what Jesus called: "Abundant Life."

Moving Beyond the Traps of Addiction AND Recovery

I was once in total bondage to drugs and alcohol and it wasn't pretty. Like so many others, my life was a tale of terrible loss and sorrow. Coming out of that life, I started out with one realization: "I was not so *smart* after all." I had to admit that I really didn't have anything "figured out" or "under control."

They said I was one of the "Lucky Ones" because I got "clean" by the age of 25. But, because I started using at age 13, I had basically wrecked my chances of having a "normal" life. I was immature. I found myself lost in an adult world filled with adult responsibilities but only having the maturity of a 13-year-old. Those vital years of growing up were lost to me because I had "checked out" both mentally and emotionally during my youth. It was a time when I should have been learning so many things!

This book is not about me, but about the ONE who made the difference in my life when so many things seemed impossible. It's about the miracles that it takes to see restoration. Like the message of God through Joel the prophet, we too can hear God say, "... I will restore to you the years that the locust has eaten." (Joel 2:25)

It is important to note here that this has not been written as a book on religion and that it's not really even a book about Christianity. The real experiences described in these pages are written to be an encouragement and the verses from the Bible that are used are presented as life-changing truth. So, for the ones wading into these pages who have given up on "religion," I ask you to read on and consider the power of real spirituality that might come through the One Who was raised from the dead!

Over the years, I have watched the Creator and Giver of Life bring hope, provide healing, and mend the broken lives of countless others. HE is the designer of all that we are, and it is only He who can fix and rebuild that which He has made! My testimony of His promise to us is this... that the God of all the universe has made a WAY through Jesus Christ to rebuild, redesign, even re-create our lives. It truly can be as if we were never broken when everything about our lives has been made brand new!

As we walk together through these pages, we will look at the way God can move us from that small, self-centered life (caused by addiction) to a life full of His presence and fruitful relationships. We will dig deep into what Jesus meant when He declared why He came, saying: "I have come that they may have life, and that they may have it more abundantly." (John 10:10)

We will look at God's Grace and how it works in the form of "divine enablement" and what it means to be "able" to do "supernaturally" that which I was "unable' to do. And, because we need to hold on to all our miracles, we will need to understand the work of Satan in our lives.

Every believer has some things that need to be "taken back" from the devil. He is a "thief" and has stolen from us all!

This book is not focused on "recovery" from addiction. It is about "Life Beyond Recovery." And, while that may sound strange to some because they view "recovery" as a place they will spend the rest of their lives, this book will take a somewhat different view.

We will look into the truth that a "born-again" believer is granted a powerful "Identity" in Christ, and that those who are born again are enabled to go beyond the "Traps" of Addiction AND Recovery. It is not only possible, but it should be considered "normal" for every born-again child of God to mature into this new Identity. Becoming a true child of God should take us to a place where the label "addict" is no longer an accurate confession of who we are!

Living in a maturing identity in Christ, we find a better confession. We discover in God's Word that we are called "saints," and "sons," and "daughters" of God. We can also discover that God intends that we have a greater freedom, no longer stuck in that wilderness place called "recovery." As we come to know our good, good Father whose intimate love sees us as dear "Children," we are enabled to embrace the "abundant life" that is more, ...so much MORE.

This book is about having faith and courage and learning to rest in Him. It is about having a God-directed sense of purpose and meaning for my life. It is about embracing an adventure with God so that I discover the joy of having a "Life Worth Living Sober."

As Children of God, we must learn to open up again and take RISK. We must begin to know what it is to make room for fruitful relationships again.

No, this book is not really about recovery from addiction. It is written for those who have felt that, even though they have learned well how to master the "tools" of "addiction recovery," there is still "more." It is for those who have become strong and stable at living "clean and sober," but still find themselves feeling miserable and thinking, "is this all there is?"

These pages are also written for the broken children of God who are still searching … for better clarity about themselves and about God. If you have worked hard to get rid of the scourge of drugs and alcohol but have yet to be settled about what you will do with your life "instead," this book is for YOU!

"Jesus said, … Get a Life!"
"I have come that they may have life, and that
they may have it more abundantly."
(John 10:10)

CHAPTER 2
Freedom

Learning To Live FREE God's Way

When faced with a tough problem, it sometimes helps to just stop, retrace our steps, and go back to the beginning. It helps to take time, clear the mind and get back to basics. When we're talking about rebuilding a life and the need for major restoration, slowing down is worth the price. Life just tends to work that way.

Rebuilding our lives will be like every challenge when we do something for the very first time. If we feel confused and like we're facing an impasse, it may be best to set the problem aside. We may need to allow some time for a change in *Perspective* or a better way of thinking.

God's Word is a powerful tool for helping us gain a better perspective like this. While many will say that that they find the Bible difficult to understand or confusing at times, it is best understood by getting first things first. It's written as a book of stories designed to help us grow. But we must get the basics and learn to build one truth upon the other.

So, to begin at "the beginning," what could be more basic than the story of the Garden of Eden? It was the place where everything began in harmony with the Creator. God designed things and made things in a place He knew was well suited for Man. God created a place of peace, and a place of joy. Yet, even in that place of perfect harmony, He told the Man, "There's still work to be done."

He said to the Man, "Be **fruitful** ... subdue (the Earth), (and) ... have dominion...." (Gen. 1:28). Mankind was not to be lazy or slothful in his efforts. He was to be like God, filled with a sense of creativity and purpose, knowing that what he DOES has value. Man was to know that he has value.

God also said something very important to the Man. It would produce a pivot-point in his experience with God. Until that moment all things were possible, nothing was conditional, and everything was GOOD. God had not yet given him rules. Certain boundaries had always existed in the mind of God, but to the Man, they were unknown.

In that place where no sin had tested the bond between the Man and his God, a boundary was necessary and God brought it to Man's attention. God said to the man, "You are 'Free' to eat from any tree in the garden; but you must not eat from the tree of the knowledge of good and evil, for when you eat from it you will certainly die." (Genesis 2:16-17 - NIV).

The freedom that man thought he understood now had a restriction placed on it and it probably felt odd.

A problem arose around this new restriction. In much the same way that all problems come about with breaking the rules, "the restriction" became the focus. Instead of the vast freedom that surrounded him, the man could only see this restriction.

God had said, "Of every tree of the garden you are Free to eat," but Adam and Eve heard something very different. The Man and his wife soon found themselves unmindful of all that was free as the serpent twisted their focus.

They soon became completely vulnerable to the serpent's guile and deception. For just like we often do, the Man and his wife had become preoccupied with restriction rather than freedom.

They could no longer live in the harmony of God's command to be creative and find purpose because they were living in the land of "Thou shalt not." God had said, "... of the tree of the knowledge of good and evil you shall NOT eat."

The curiosity toward that which was "forbidden" coupled with the taunting dare of a deceiver had made them lose sight of the great blessing God had provided. He had said, "You are 'Free' to eat from any tree in the garden." But there in the midst of perfect provision, perfect harmony, and the perfect Love of their Creator, they lost sight of His goodness and the life of bliss that was theirs.

Hasn't this same drama played out many times in our own lives as well? Haven't we at times found ourselves in a bondage of our own doing? This is precisely how we lost sight of all that was good, and free, and abundant; it is the most basic problem we all face. It is that loss of focus over some negative experience that so easily causes our downward spiral into rebellion and sin.

Just like Adam and Eve, our downfall begins when our focus deviates toward some forbidden thing or perceived loss. We so easily lose sight of the blessing and the freedom God gives us.

If we would only choose to live within His boundaries, His abundance would always be available. Yet, those who still hear His voice and heed His call know that we were made to be "fruitful, subdue the earth, and have dominion."

So many of us have lost things that God intended us to enjoy in Freedom. Whether it be the loss of family relationships, finances, or simply our peace of mind, it all began when we lost our focus on His Goodness. Perhaps we thought that "Thou shalt not" was a big deal, something intended to keep us from having "fun." We probably did just like the man and woman in the garden and walked right into Satan's trap!

What You See Is What You Are

The journey back to Abundant Life is not some easy "walk in the park" for most of us. It will be an experience filled with challenges and potholes, and some bumps in the road. But one thing that removes some of the difficulty is taking a long, healthy look at myself.

We've all heard that how we see ourselves can have a powerful effect on what we become. It's common knowledge that a healthy self image, opens up new possibilities while a poor self-image can be as crippling as being in chains.

For many it's as if those "chains" are completely invisible. Many of us are going though life bound with chains we don't even know are there. Others may be living as if they are still bound when Jesus has already set them free.

The most fundamental principle for rebuilding a life after being set free from addiction is simply to **KNOW you are free**!

Understanding Freedom will require a deeper spiritual insight. It requires faith in the *"finished work of Christ."* When we look into that mirror, we must be able to see Him and the new *image* He has made for us. It must be applied to every area of our lives.

We must refuse to be double-minded about it. Knowing that I am free means that I understand what I am not. I am not "someone in bondage trying to get free." I must see myself as someone who is "FREE" shaking off some "bondage!" I must "see" through the eyes of my *new identity*!

Walking in this freedom means that I stop living by *the natural creed* that says, "Hello my name is _____, and I'm an addict." I must begin living by the *supernatural creed* that says: "… if anyone *is* in Christ, *he is* a **new creation**; old things have passed away; behold, all things have become **new**" (2 Corinthians 5:17).

Taking on this new identity and self-image, means that I *believe* that Christ has done *all* that was necessary. His provision alone has done everything needed to restore *all* that Adam lost!

It Has Never Been "Enough" Just To Stay "Clean"

When I look myself in the face, I can not give sway to the intoxicating emotions of self-pity and the "*poor, poor me's*." I can no longer wallow in my sadness in hopes that some co-dependent soul will wallow in it with me. Walking in this freedom requires that I kick that "*victim mentality*" out for good and draw deep from the Spirit of God for something greater.

This Freedom only comes to those who will dig deep to discover the person that I once was and the person "in Christ" I am to become. True Freedom belongs to those who will not stop until the enabling grace of God has empowered them to discover the fullness of identity that God gave at *the beginning*.

This journey of freedom is about rebuilding *"a life worth living sober."* It has never been enough to settle for *"staying clean."* It has never been enough just to get "my family and my stuff back." It will never be enough even if I learn to "give sobriety away to others."

We have all known people who have achieved those things only to hit one of life's *potholes* and end up in a ditch. We can settle for no less than TOTAL TRANSFORMATION in Christ and a reshaping of everything we thought we knew.

"Of every tree" (the good things of God) ... WE ARE FREE to partake and enjoy His abundance! This is freedom restored. It is a place beyond *recovery* that takes us into *restoration*.

It is a place where I begin to look in the mirror and see myself as He created me to be. This is the freedom to "be *fruitful*, to *subdue* every enemy, and to have *dominion*" as He intended (Genesis 1:28).

It is the freedom to begin *taking back my life* from the enemy. It is where I learn that the safest, most abundant place in the world lies within God's boundaries. He is the good, good God who made me and the only One who can put me back together!

"Jesus said, ... Get a Life!"
"I have come that they may have life, and that they may have it more abundantly."
(John 10:10)

CHAPTER 3

Expectation

Getting Rid of the "Have-Nots" and Negativity

Merriam Webster's Dictionary defines the word "optimism" is: "anticipating the best possible outcome." And, while "faith" is certainly more than that, we know that an element of faith involves having an "expectation" towards God and His goodness. We don't have to look very far to see that the world is filled with a viral form of "negativity." It just seems to spread and taint everything that it touches. Getting rid of the "have not" mentality will require that we resist and repel this negativity that surrounds us.

Sometimes we aren't aware just how deep this negative flow has penetrated inside of us. It can leave us scarred and disillusioned. We become cynical and judgmental and it can easily get so bad that we lose our way into a dark, dark place. The world we once knew seems unrecognizable in this place and when we look at ourselves all we see is a distorted resemblance of who we once were.

I was in such a place in the summer of 1983. It was a long time ago, but I remember that dark, cynical place and I remember just how one loving and positive moment spun me around and brought me out of it, at least for a while.

None of the things that used to bring me comfort and joy seemed a part of my life in those days. I was still young but only a shell of the man I was meant to be. It was Father's Day and I had my 2½-year-old daughter for the weekend. Divorced, broken, in poor health and hanging by a thread to stay clean and sober, I was living back at home with my parents.

I wasn't quite yet 24 years old and I felt like 40. The drugs and party lifestyle I had lived since I was around 13 years old had left a fog in my brain and my maturity was stunted. Cynicism was my middle name. And like a grumpy old man, I spent my days being critical of others and pushing people away.

My best days were spent analyzing what was wrong with the world and sometimes telling others just how useless and stupid everything was. I was sober alright, ... but still miserable and I didn't have a clue how to break out of the wet blanket I had wrapped around myself.

My mother woke me that Father's Day Sunday and announced it was time to get ready for church.

Our family had always gone to church; but, for me, it had become mostly a place where I could only feel shame and condemnation. I had ruined my own life. I had torn apart my family with my own hands and everybody in my hometown knew it.

Seeing that I was less than enthusiastic about going to church, Mom suggested that I take my daughter with me to visit the little church where "Larry" was the Pastor. Larry had been one of the few people in town that never made me feel condemned and had reached out to me in love.

It was a beautiful day in early June filled with sunshine and my daughter and I actually enjoyed the drive out to Larry's little country church. The people there were always so friendly and you could tell that this young pastor had helped them learn to be that way. It was a place of peace and joy.

Right after the singing part of the service was finished, Pastor Larry stepped to the pulpit and said, "Today is a very special day when we want to celebrate all our fathers and we have some gifts we want to give you Dads." He was actually grinning from ear to ear and just seemed to glow with this heavenly kind of joy. This man was actually thrilled and excited about celebrating visitors and about fathers and just about everything he talked about.

As he proceeded with his plans to give out gifts to the fathers, my mind began to wander as happens to people sometimes in church. But I was suddenly stunned back into focus towards what was going on in the room when I heard him say, "how about you, young man, how old are you?" I didn't realize that after they gave a gift to the "oldest" father in the room, they were now looking for the youngest.

The pastor said, "Is that your daughter?" I was holding her in my arms and when I realized he was speaking to me I just said, "Yes, she is." He then said something that literally pulled a piece of my soul right out of that dark, dark place. He said, "Well, how wonderful! I bet you are so proud to be her Daddy. She is just beautiful!"

I stood there, staring around the room at this church full of smiling faces. They just looked like they truly loved me and were happy I was there. There was no shame, no condemnation, and no room to be cynical in that moment. And right there it occurred to me, "I am PROUD to be her Daddy. And, she is BEAUTIFUL!"

These loving Christians then gave me their gift for being the youngest father and they just celebrated me like I was something special. I will never forget that day because, for a moment in time, I was able to see that, in Christ, I don't have to be ashamed of my past, and, in Him, I will never be condemned. These people didn't know that I had been a drug addict. They knew nothing of my past, of a child conceived out of wedlock, of my divorce, or any of the "Negative" things that I carried with me.

It was that day that I first began to get a glimpse of just how self-defeating self pity can be. I had been in so deep, wallowing in my "poor, poor me's" that I didn't even know how to see what a precious gift my beautiful daughter was (and to this day, she really is beautiful). I was so buried in my "have nots" that I couldn't begin to see all the wonderful things that I already "had."

Jesus said, "...everyone who has, ...will have in abundance." We cannot even begin to understand what that truly means if our focus is always on what we "don't have." For many of us, our breakthrough into new maturity and abundance will only come when we confront the "*cynical spirit*" we have embraced.

But coming out of the darkness isn't complete with just a "glimpse" of the Light. A revelation of how cynical we have become is just the beginning of our battle. We will need to step into some specific "haves" that will empower us with some of heaven's resources. We will need to "have" some faith, and "have" some courage. We will need to start believing in God's abundance and "have" some confidence that in Christ we will "have" all we need to overcome!

A Revelation of "Benefits," and a Leap of Faith

I will never forget when The Holy Spirit first dropped into my spirit a revelation of Psalm 103:2-5:

"Bless the Lord, O my soul, And forget not all His benefits: Who forgives all your iniquities, Who heals all your diseases, Who redeems your life from destruction, Who crowns you with lovingkindness and tender mercies, Who satisfies your mouth with good things, So that your youth is renewed like the eagle's."

I remember thinking, "My relationship with God is FULL OF BENEFITS!" Let me tell you, for a cynical man, that's some good news. I wasn't used to thinking of God as a great benefactor. He was the one who sat in judgment. He had this very long list of Do's and Don't's and may have, in fact, been the only person grumpier than I was!

For me, this was a brand-new way of looking at God. And, perhaps the greatest thing about this new revelation was the simple approach these verses suggested was the way into these benefits. It said, "Bless the Lord oh my soul and forget NOT all His benefits."

That was the day that I first began my journey to engage God in His covenant. He was inviting me to participate in something. All I had to do to get started was to "bless the Lord" deeply from my soul and SAY that He is good and that He wants good things for me!

Faith does not begin with a revelation of my need. It begins when we are overwhelmed by the love and the goodness of a God who would see me in sin, take my punishment, and then chase me down to pour out His benefits.

The only faith that has power to change things is the faith that comes from God and is like the faith OF God. His kind of faith has the power to SAY, "Let there be ..." and it was so. His faith is never mustered or conjured up by misguided motives but is always pure, loving, and aimed at goodness.

The benefits of God come to those who dare to learn the God kind of faith. This faith must see an outcome. It must "give" something in response to God (sowing a seed) and it must engage God with an investment so great that there is no turning back. We have all been given lives filled with choices. And, as believers, we have access to benefits from God that never run out through His spiritual resources.

When we are invested in His Kingdom to the point of no return, faith takes over because we have left ourselves no other way out. There is no back door through which to escape back to the world. If our problem has been having one foot "in" and one foot "out" of God's Kingdom, the only solution is obvious. We must jump in with both feet abandoning all else. Then, when it frightens us as if we just jumped off a cliff, that will be the moment we will know what faith truly is.

Getting Rid of the "Have Nots" of Negativity

"For to everyone who has, more will be given, and he will have abundance; but from him who does not have, even what he has will be taken away." (Matthew 25:29)

As young believers, many of us may have read this statement with a puzzled look on our faces. Why would our loving, giving, and gracious Jesus say such a thing. It almost sounds like He's saying that the "Have's" of this world will be given more and the "have nots" will have the little that they have taken away. Wait a minute, that IS exactly what He is saying, in a certain sense.

Reading the entire section of Matthew 25 (verses 14 through 30) opens up the insight Jesus meant for us through a story about a wealthy man who went on a journey and gave his servants gifts. The story goes on to tell us that two of the three servants traded or invested these gifts and from that investment made a profit. But one of them hid his gift and did nothing to make it grow.

Then Jesus tells us that the wealthy man returned to settle accounts with his servants. The first two had invested or put to use their gifts and, having shown their master their return on investment, were told, "Well done!" But the servant with the one gift who went and hid the gift was told something very different.

He came to settle his account with his master full of excuses. He said he "was afraid" and hid his master's gift in the ground. He tried to present it back to him as if not "losing" the gift and giving it back in tact was the best he could do. Perhaps expecting to hear praise as the others had heard, he was probably shocked when the master said to him, "You wicked and lazy servant ... you ought to have deposited my money with the bankers, and at my coming I would have received back my own with interest."

And just before the verse quoted at the beginning of this chapter, we have an astounding statement. Jesus tells us that the master of the "fearful" servant said, "... take the talent from him, and give *it* to him who has ten talents." THAT is when Jesus says, "For to everyone who has, more will be given, and he will have abundance; but from him who does not have, *even what he has* will be taken away." (Matthew 25:29)

But why? I remember wondering about this as a young man first reading the Bible for myself. Why would Jesus be advocating that they take what little the poor man has and give it to the man who has already made a handsome profit for himself?

I have learned over the years that the natural eyes and the natural mind cannot receive or understand the complete answer. It is because anyone whose explanation is limited to the resources of the natural world cannot see it. It is because, in our minds, the resources of this world are limited and earthbound. We cannot see beyond our scarcity mentality.

Like starving men wrestling over the pieces of a dwindling pie, most people live out their lives in fear, unable or unwilling to take the risk to invest. And just like in the parable, though the seed or the money to invest is a gift from someone else, we still find ourselves either too fearful or too lazy to step out in faith.

The answer will only be found by those who dare to look deeply into exactly what Jesus means in His story by the words, *"everyone who **HAS***!*"* Far from the mentality of scarcity and the soulish fears of lazy indecision is a place of ABUNDANCE. It is a place where spiritual men and women learn to draw from a BANK of heavenly resources that never run out. It is a place where new boldness and confidence is found and where every thought of risk is embraced in the comfort of knowing that even when there's loss, there is always MORE.

What Is That in Your Hand?

The man Moses is remembered by most as a "mighty man of miracles" in the Bible who stood up to the great king, Pharaoh. But it was not always that way with Moses. His beginnings, in fact, were anything but "mighty" during a part of his life where he murdered an Egyptian and ran away, hiding in fear for his life. (Genesis, Chapters 2-3)

There on the back side of a desert in the region of Midian, Moses, already in the latter years of his life, had a visitation from God. After God tells Moses that he is calling him to be a "deliverer" of Israel and that God plans to give the Israelites "favor" with the Egyptians to let them go, Moses says to God:

> *"But suppose they will not believe me or listen to my voice; suppose they say, ''The Lord has not appeared to you.' and the Lord said to him, 'What is that in your hand?' He said, 'A rod.' And He said, 'Cast it on the ground.'"* (Genesis 4:1-3)

While it is easy for us to think of this rod as little more than a common stick, it was far more than that to Moses. This was the symbol of his livelihood. God was asking Moses to yield and lay before Him the thing on which Moses depended most. He was a Shepherd and that rod was the tool by which he tended the sheep.

It was only when Moses had invested with this act of surrender and laid down that rod that he began to see the "miracles" he was born to produce. The Bible says that when he cast it down "it became a serpent" so dreadful that at first Moses "fled from it." But in a matter of moments, that same fearful Moses reached out his hand and took that serpent by the tail at the command of God and it became a rod again (Genesis 4:3-4). It was in this way that an investment of obedience began a great covenant journey for Moses and the people of Israel!

How Much Do You Have?

It was also in this fashion that the first disciples learned a powerful lesson. An experience with Jesus taught them that the eyes of faith can see much more than what meets the eye (Mark 6:35-42). As was His custom, Jesus had ministered long that day till those that helped Him had reached the end of their resources. They felt tired and began to worry that so many "needy" people were around them in a remote and deserted place. These people were hungry and had nothing to eat!

The disciples suggested that Jesus "send them away" so they could "buy themselves bread." But the inexhaustible Jesus stretched the disciples even further when He said, "You give them something to eat." Then, as they began to busy themselves with counting the money they could find, Jesus asked them, "How many loaves do you have?"

It was a question much like the one that God had asked Moses. The answer to the situation did not rest in what they actually had, but in the faith with which they gave it.

The meager five loaves and two fish that came forth after they counted probably did not seem like the answer Jesus wanted. But, after what was probably a sheepish presentation of their small provision, the Bible says that "... *when (Jesus) had taken the five loaves and the two fish, He looked up to heaven, blessed and broke the loaves, and gave them to His disciples to set before them; and the two fish He divided among them all. So they all ate and were filled.*" (Mark 6:41-42)

Since verse 44 goes on to tell us that those who had eaten that day were about "five thousand men," we can know with certainty that the God kind of faith was at work. Jesus had reached His faith-filled hands into the abundant resources of heaven and pulled out a meal for over 5,000 people counting women and children. The circumstances were dramatically changed because His eyes of faith had seen beyond the natural realm of earth.

If we really want to move from a small, self-centered life to living in fullness and shared abundance, it has to start with getting our eyes wide open to the resources of heaven. Nothing else that I might try towards rebuilding my life out of the ruins can jumpstart the process like learning this one principle.

Living in the "have-nots" will keep me trapped in the place of "never enough." But, if I will learn to *release* to God with an open hand whatever it is He asks of me; and if I will learn to *receive* from Him the exact supernatural provision for every challenge, I cannot lose!

This is where I begin to see HOW the Spirit of God enables me to take back what the devil stole from me and even MORE. A lot can change when I begin to live by the rules of God's economy. Opening my eyes to His race and resources will empower me to blow the lid off the limitations that have kept me bound.

If I will learn to live this way, it will be like I had suddenly turned a key that opens a door into a "life worth living sober."

"Jesus said, ... Get a Life!"
"I have come that they may have life, and that
they may have it more abundantly."
(John 10:10)

CHAPTER 4

Identity

Who Am I and Why Am I Here?

*It's NOT "climbing the ladder" but choosing the
"Wall" that matters*

I once heard someone tell an interesting story about a man climbing "the ladder of success." He told of how each rung of the ladder represented milestones in the man's life and how he had overcome obstacles to keep on climbing. Since the story was told during a leadership training, it was easy to assume that the point was about how "perseverance" or "determination" had enabled the man to reach the top of the ladder.

Then, just as it should be when stories are told with a punch line that imprints the main point on your memory, the totally unexpected happened. The storyteller got to the part where the man on the ladder was almost at the top. As he made the transition in telling his story from the ladder to the conclusion of the climb, he suddenly blurted out, "but upon reaching his goal at the top of the ladder, the man discovered a problem that he had not seen. He had climbed alright, better than anyone else around him, but in utter disillusionment, he screamed, 'All this time, my ladder was on the WRONG WALL!'"

So many things in life can be like that story. It can be disheartening to expend so much energy trying to make a change or accomplish success only to find that it's not "climbing the ladder" but choosing the "wall" that matters. Setting our sights on the right goals at the right time isn't always easy, but it's worth slowing down a little to sharpen our focus. How many times have we raced on ahead with an idea only to find that all the effort in the world wouldn't have made the outcome better. If a thing is not in line with God's will, sometimes the failure of it IS a "success" (anyone remember Abraham and his Ishmael?).

Trying to move beyond "Recovery" into "Rebuilding" a quality Life God's way can be a lot like that. So many have spent a lot of energy focused on all the things that people tell them will keep them "sober," but never get around to focusing on the things that will get them "changed." But God is in the "changing" business, especially the kind of change that makes things "new." Having the "ladder" on the right "wall" when it comes to a restored life means getting my focus on the issues at the core. It will mean spending some time and energy on rebuilding "my identity from heaven's resources."

It's Not the Crime, but the Cover-Up That Gets You!

A very important part of the "Eden" story in Genesis gives us an illustration of what happens when we are alienated from God. What happened to them is what happens to us. The same way that Adam and Eve got caught up in a drama they did not intend, you and I share this same experience of "nakedness" and "hiding." In our shame, we, just like Adam and Eve, often create our coverings of "fig leaves" that do little more than mark us as those who have lost something they once were.

This episode in the life of Adam and Eve is told as follows:

"Then the eyes of both of them were opened, and they knew that they were naked; and they **sewed fig leaves** *together and* **made themselves coverings***. And they heard the sound of the LORD God walking in the garden in the cool of the day, and Adam and his wife hid themselves from the presence of the LORD God among the trees of the garden. Then the LORD God called to Adam and said to him, 'Where are you?' So he said, 'I heard Your voice in the garden, and* **I was afraid** *because* **I was naked***; and* **I hid myself***.'" (and)*

*"... for Adam and his wife the LORD **God made tunics of skin, and clothed them.**" (Genesis 3:7-10 & 21)*

Their story is recorded for us to demonstrate the unintended consequences of taking matters into our own hands. It is a picture of those places in life where we have said to God, at least indirectly, "I'll be the judge of that." This same story plays out again and again in our lives as we make "choices" that lead to "consequences" that lead to "fig leaves" that leave us hiding from the only One who can make things right.

But the damage done is not limited to the loss created through alienation and hiding. More than just a little "trauma" and more than just a little "twisting" of our lives can be brought about through just one initial act of rebellion. It can be like tipping that first domino in a long line of effects. The damage cannot be measured by that first "tip" when it is clearly the chain reaction that follows that is Satan's desired result!

Alcoholism and addiction never take place in a vacuum. Anyone who tries to tell you they can explain the dynamics of addiction with "one-size-fits-all" approach is just blowing smoke. It is NOT just that there are many things that come into play in the making of an addictive profile and personality. The challenge is that EVERYTHING in and about a person's life has an impact and can bear influence into the "dynamics" of a person's addiction.

The only thing "simple" about addiction is this: The addiction of every addict has four basic components or phases - 1) A choice that creates a starting point, 2) a focal point of Rebellion before God, 3) A cover up (fig leaves - basically Satan-inspired defense mechanisms that distort the personality), and 4) A set of unbearable consequences allowed into our lives to awaken us to the TRUTH. We must discover that only He can cover our shame and put us back together.

The Lost "Self" That Was Meant To BE

The "fig leaves" in the Garden with God involved a lot more than an effort to cover nakedness and shame. The first man and woman must have been horrified at what had really changed. Their eyes were opened to a stark reality and something had been LOST. Where was His Presence? Where was the Light of His Glory that once had covered them? Theirs was now a life experience entirely haunted by the aching God-shaped hole at the center of their being. If things were to ever get better, it would only happen because they found "Him," and found themselves again.

What they had not understood was that the cost of rebellion was never really measured by their eyes being opened or by realizing they were "naked." The Serpent had tempted them with dreams of being wise and with the promise of "being like God." Nothing like that actually happened. The consequence of rebellion against God overtook them the same as it overtakes you and me. When the "fig leaves" of addiction begin to take their toll, we lose a part of ourselves. They lost their former self as we have lost ours and we will only find our way back "home" if we surrender to Him who makes all things new.

Inside of each of us, no matter the damage we have suffered, lies the seed of the "child" we once were as God intended us to be. Our God who is never bound by time or place can reach back to the innocent child we once were and make us again, in His image, a New Man or a New Woman. Better still, He that "makes all things new" is able through Christ to give us His Spirit and transform us into someone who shines like the Lord, Himself.

Heaven's Resources and A New Identity

The Bible says in I Corinthians 15:22, 45, and 48-49:

*"For as **in Adam all die**, even so **in Christ all shall be made alive**…"*

*"And so it is written, 'The **first man Adam** became a living **being**.' The **last Adam** became a life-giving **spirit**…"*

*"As was the **man of dust**, so also are those who are **made of dust**; and as is the **heavenly Man**, so also are **those who are heavenly**. And as we have borne the **image of the man of dust**, we shall also bear the **image of the heavenly Man**."*

This "image of the heavenly Man" is very enlightening and tells us a lot about what God is actually doing. From this word "image," or the Greek, *"eikŏn"* we are given an expression of something much like the passing on of a source-code very similar to DNA. From what we know about DNA, it functions like a pattern or design code for replication of certain traits. It is what gives us our look, our design, and, to some degree, our personality.

This word *"eikŏn"* or "image" (of the heavenly Man) is describing for us a built-in, miraculous principle that is given through the Spirit of Christ to "REPLICATE" His image into our lives! *"Eikŏn"* is defined as: "An image that exactly reflects its source. It does not merely resemble the source but is drawn from it, a replication." *"We shall also bear the IMAGE of the Heavenly Man!"* (I Corinthians. 15:49)

That twisted, fallen and distorted version of me that was my "old man" is something of death and dust and is only fit for death and burial. It is to be PUT OFF and left for dead as we die to that old self born of bad choices, rebellion, fig leaves (Satan-inspired defense mechanisms), and a life-long pattern of unbearable consequences.

Our New Identity will not come about through the efforts of mind, will, emotion or flesh. All the tools in our too-belt for staying clean & sober, all the knowledge we have about avoiding triggers and managing our thoughts may someday wear thin and fail us.

Only one complete and thorough overhaul of the self can provide us with the resources we need for total transformation that will last a lifetime. We must be reborn spiritually through Christ in such a way that our whole identity is reformed in us.

The Unyielding Strength of Being a Child of God

Answering the question, "Who am I and why am I here?" becomes much easier for the child of God who knows God's Word and learns to hear His voice. It is the fundamental RIGHT of every believer to experience a re-birth of their identity through Christ. And, the first rule of receiving all that is mine in Him is to LISTEN for His voice believing that I AM WHO HE SAYS I AM!

Unfortunately, the world is full of voices that will contradict what God says about me, and sometimes my own self-condemnation is the worst offender! We all have to learn to agree with God immediately when a new revelation of His goodness towards us is breaks through to our hearts and minds. Satan, himself, is the master of condemnation and the Bible calls him, "The Accuser of the Brethren."

Our Father God, on the other hand, is always saying good and loving things toward us. When we stand before Him in our faith in Christ, His Word to us is: "For I know the plans I have for you," declares the LORD, "plans to prosper you and not to harm you, plans to give you **hope and a future**." (Jeremiah 29:11)

Since the Bible teaches that "**death and life** *are* in the **power of the tongue**" (Prov. 18:21), it is important that we train our mouths to speak in agreement with God. Since the enemy of my soul is always out to "steal, kill, and destroy" (the other part of John 10:10), I must use my faith and my words to speak in agreement with God believing Him for my destiny and for my prosperity. By faith, I can declare and speak forth the change that God says He wants in my life.

Finally, since forming a New Identity in me is God's idea in the first place, I can know that He wants to complete it. So, if there are difficulties along the way or if progress seems slow, I can know that the problem is NOT with God. Sometimes our progress in transformation is held back by strongholds that still need to be broken. Other times, we may easily see the pace pick up when we sever old "soul ties" that should not be there or step up in our faithfulness and obedience. I must be willing to remove anything in my life that may be a hindrance to seeing God's new inner image of myself and believing it.

Walking steady with God on this journey of rebuilding the life He wants for me can be a beautiful thing. As the Great Designer/Creator of all things, God is the logical helper for putting things back in order. Through His Spirit in us, God will impart to us a new strength in the personality we were meant to have. Only He is able to pour into us spiritual gifts and callings that will speak to our innermost being and call forth our destiny and purpose.

"Who am I and why am I here?" One thing is for sure, I am not here to wallow in the consequences of a fallen existence from bad choices and live under the shadow of "fig leaves" that twist and distort the person I was meant to be. I am a Child of The Living God! Anything less than the fulfillment of His promises and spending out my days in the satisfying occupation of His calling and purpose is far too low for me. I AM who He says I AM! And, tapping into that source for my identity will definitely produce "A Life Worth Living Sober."

"Jesus said, ... Get a Life!"
"I have come that they may have life, and that
they may have it more abundantly."
(John 10:10)

CHAPTER 5

Connections

Why Relationships Matter

Profile of a "Winner"
I Samuel 17

The Philistine armies were gathered together between Sochoh and Azekah. Saul and Israel had gathered to meet them in the Valley of Elah. The battle array was drawn where both armies faced each other, mountain facing mountain, with a valley in the middle.

A cry came from the Philistine side as they shouted his name, "Goliath, Goliath" and a cold shiver went up the spines of the Israelites. Covered in bronze with a javelin and sword like no other, a shield-bearer went before the giant frame in confidence that the battle was won.

The Champion stood and cried out that a man of the Israelites should be CHOSEN to come out to face him. There was no need for these armies to fight. It could all be settled by two men, one from each army. He began to shout blasphemies and taunted them saying, "I defy the armies of Israel this day!"

What reply could Israel give? There was no man in Israel that could take this monster! In dismay the Israelites camped there hoping, praying that God would send them a miracle. For forty days and nights the Philistine Champion mocked them with no reply. These were dark days for Israel as their hearts began to conform to the image the giant predicted for them: "you shall be our slaves and you shall serve us!"

But the youngest son of an Ephrathite from Bethlehem, Judah finally arrived simply obeying his father on a mission to deliver loaves and cheese. He was but a boy. He had no skill as a soldier, no armor, no sword. The only thing he knew was herding sheep and the simple weapons used for killing animals that threatened the sheep.

When he arrived, he saw the Philistine and heard the commotion of Israel's warriors. He saw them cowered and hiding behind the rocks. And as the soldiers expressed their horror and intimidation to the boy they mentioned that THE KING had made a PROMISE for the man who killed the giant. THE KING "will enrich him with great riches," they said, "and will give him his daughter, and give his father's house exemption from taxes."

With the heart of a winner, this young boy named David had only one response to the circumstances before him. His identity was clear and strong that day; and with the confidence of a son of God, David rose up and shouted, "Who is this uncircumcised Philistine, that he should defy the armies of the living God?"

When David was taken before the King of Israel, David declared to the King, "I have killed both the lion and the bear; and this uncircumcised Philistine will be like one of them, seeing he has defied the armies of the living God." David knew His God, and through confidence in his covenant relationship with Him, he knew HOW TO ENGAGE GOD IN THE BATTLE AND WIN!

With only five stones and a shepherd's sling in his hand, David drew near to the Philistine. Then with taunts, disdain and cursing the giant declared to David that he would "feed his flesh to the birds and the beasts."

The shepherd boy stood calm and, with no fear in his heart, made his declaration over his enemy: "You come to me with a sword, ... But I come to you in the name of the Lord of Hosts, the God of the armies of Israel, whom you have defied. This day the Lord will deliver you into my hand ..."

Moments later God had done through the most unlikely, the most unassuming child what the mighty men of Israel could not do that day. Not only did David sink that stone into the giant's forehead with one shot of his sling, but he stood over his foe in the most valiant sign of victory.

THIS is what covenant looks like. THIS is what winning against all odds looks like! Can you imagine the shock on the faces of the king and his soldiers that day when they saw this shepherd boy standing over the enemy's champion with the giant's sword in one hand and the giant's head in the other?

The important thing for us is this: we have a decision to make. Is this just some bed-time story made up like a fairy tale to give children hope as they drift off to sleep? Or, is this story REAL, given to us to illustrate the kind of overcoming, covenant relationship we should have with our Father God? The truth is that the Bible and its battle-stories that teach us how to WIN are not for "sissies." But it CAN help us learn to fight again and learn to win again when the darkness of the world has left us defeated and hopeless.

My Choices, my Destiny ... My Father's Dreams

Forging a relationship with God that produces a "faith-confidence" does not happen by itself. It will not come to those who engage in "passive religion' or rise in the hearts of timid and cowardly souls. A spiritual warrior's victory will only be had by the warrior's heart. It can be learned and it can be sought. But it will only be found by one who would dare cry out for "more" from God, by the one who longs for "*intimacy.*"

Too many of us have settled for less than God's best because we have been taught to understand Biblical stories through a false lens of "sovereignty and destiny." People will say, "David was God's chosen vessel and was able to do great things because it was God's sovereign will." We are told that such miraculous victories and power don't "normally" happen in our lives but are the result of being "chosen and having a special destiny from God."

But, what about the "choices" WE make? What about the side of David's story that tells us He CULTIVATED great faith through long hours of worship and time spent with God? Is it possible that great things happen in the lives of people who CHOOSE to cultivate great faith? Could it be that a part of God's own "choosing" of us has to do with whether or not we make ourselves a good and faithful choice?

Biblical sovereignty and destiny are something totally different from the fatalism that views God as a great "puppet master." A view of God's sovereignty that resigns itself to the phrase "whatever will be, will be" is simply NOT BIBLICAL!

The God Who tells us about Himself throughout the Bible has always expressed Himself as One who "engages" with us in relationship. He also longs for us to "engage" with Him. Real relationships are not dictated by one party to the other, but must be free. It is this kind of freedom that God gives when He acknowledges the will of man. This is an important way that love operates between us and God. Our freedom in the relationship with God helps us define what true love is.

Our "destiny" from God, rather than being a "plan" dictated from His throne, is really more of a "dream" born out of His heart. Like any good Father, our Father God has "dreams" for His children that are born from His heart to ours.

And, while this dream of our Father's heart is often revealed to us as His will for our lives, it is still up to us to embrace the "dream" by faith. In this way, my life-purpose becomes more than just a "job to do." It is a privilege and an invitation to a lifelong "dance." As we embrace the "dream" and engage in the "dance," our faith enables His will to become our reality.

Yes, David had a calling, a destiny born in the heart of Father God. David was able to tap into that vision for his life and fulfill it because he knew the Father's heart. Such destiny is never just a "given" and it can always be derailed.

Just like David, you and I can tap into the Father's dreams for us. Our "destiny" comes out of the heart of a Father who loves us. And, we can know that He always dreams of GOOD things for us **(Jeremiah 29:11).** God has plans for us, *"plans to prosper ... not to harm ..., and plans to give us hope and a future."*

And there will be many CHOICES to make along the way. The outcome of our lives and the fulfillment of our destiny will rise and fall on the faith we cultivate in our relationship with God. Like David we must view our future like a crop that will surely come at that pivotal moment in time. We will know it when it starts to happen because we will see a miraculous faith begin to rise to its victorious occasion.

Your Level of Relationship Really Matters

Our relationship with God is often illustrated in the Bible by some picture of the Marriage Covenant or a story that depicts one of the challenges of marriage. The power of covenant is illustrated again and again by God's love and faithfulness as the ultimate "bridegroom."

We can see this demonstrated in the relationship between God and His People throughout the Bible. God refers to His people as His "Bride" (Isaiah 62:5), gives Israel a certificate of "divorce" (Jeremiah 3:8), and in the New Testament, Paul uses a "marriage" to illustrate "Christ and the church" (Ephesians 5:29-32).

The Marriage relationship is the greatest illustration of a "covenant commitment" that we have and can be a beautiful portrayal of a spiritual connection. Husbands and wives are intended to have a great bond of trust that is forged in fires of accountability and learning to rely on one another.

A relationship with God is really no different. Why should we think that a covenant with God will develop out of just giving God a little time on Sunday morning? People often say they "believe" and want to call a little church-going a relationship with God. Yet James tells us that even the demons "believe" and "tremble" but that doesn't mean they know God at all (James 2:19).

We so often want our prayers answered and our miracles received with very little effort expended to "exercise" faith or "execute" the will of God. The problem is that Jesus left us His will and testament and made us the "executor" of His will. Yet, we often just sit around whining and complaining about how "God really should do something!"

What we don't understand is that HE DID DO all that He needed to do. He made a way through the resurrected Christ for us to "execute" His will in the earth by the *authority* He gave us (Luke 10:19). We miss out on so much of what is ours just because we don't fully engage in the covenant we have with Him. Our problem is that we have yet to make a clear and radical CHOICE to surrender to His will and begin to DO our part.

Reconnecting Will Often Require Great Humility

If we want restoration, if we want to truly rebuild our lives from the ruins, we will need to be more like the prodigal son (Luke 15). Yes, he was wasteful and riotous and did all the things many of us did that brought shame and disrespect on our families. But he did one thing that brought a pivot point to his circumstances. It changed everything and turned things around.

He made a decision to humble himself and *go HOME*. The prodigal chose to submit to His Father's will. The Bible says in Luke 15:17 that "he *came to himself*" and said, (v.18) "I will arise and go to my Father and say, 'Father I have sinned.'" The phrase "he came to himself" tells us that he had lost his very identity.

To come to one's self means that you reconnect with a "self" you had lost. You realize that you somehow, somewhere have left your "self" behind. It is the restoration of God-given identity. It requires a return to that place where the twisted version of the self came about and exposing it for what it is. It is coming out of the fantasy and waking up from the nightmare.

Nothing changed until the prodigal DID something about it. He got up, chose to go home, and chose to confess that he had done wrong. The way he drew near to his Father and stepped up to clear his conscience is exactly what we will need to do.

We have to come to a new level of engagement with God. No covenant left "unengaged" will ever be enforced or have the power to bring us benefit. If we want the benefits and the promises we will have to engage the relationship!

Our relationship with Father God is clouded and weak when our conscience is not clear. It is very difficult to experience a real change when we are unwilling to "clear the air" and remove things that block the relationship. Our "faith" can only be as good as the quality of our relationship, and our relationship with God will only be as good as the effort we make to attend to it.

1 John 3:21 says, *"Beloved, if our heart does not **condemn** us, we have CONFIDENCE toward God."* It is this "confidence" before God that fortifies our faith to *"receive"* what we need through our prayers. Like David, only "confidence" will give us the resolve and connection we need through the Spirit to be free from "doubt."

The Bible tells us that getting rid of doubt is really important. James 1:6-8 says that *"... he who doubts is like a wave of the sea driven and tossed by the wind. For let not that man suppose that he will receive anything from the Lord; he is a double-minded man, unstable in all his ways."*

To "engage God in covenant" means to come to him in surrender, ready to choose Him and forsake all others. It means leaving ourselves no back door or way of "escape." An engaged, covenant believer is a Christian who is ready to do his or her part to turn things around and see things get better.

Rebuilding a life requires some hard work and the first order of business is to flush out anything that is trashing up our relationship with God. Then, when we make our efforts to connect with Him, our faith will flow like the streams of "living water" it was meant to be.

Then There Were THREE, the Covenant Extended

Having our relationship restored and learning to live "connected" with God is a huge step towards the rebuilding of our lives. Yet being reconnected with God is only the beginning of this journey into the kind of relational, covenant living that brings "abundant life."

God laid down a principle for Adam in the book of Genesis that being "alone" was NOT "good" (Gen. 2:18).

In fact, it was the very first thing God ever said was not "good" in His new creation. The Creator expressed His intention when He created "Eve" that Man was to live out his "abundance" in the context of relationship. He was to have a "Helper," but learning to receive the "help" first required that He also learn to "give."

Nothing would ever shape, express, or test the character of the man like the necessity of sharing his life with another. Nothing else would be so capable of showing the man how his actions could grieve the heart of God when he sinned. He would need to learn how to love her. He would be accountable. And, he would have to feel what it is to offer grace and forgiveness. He would better understand why he sought to be forgiven.

Without GRACE, the Covenant Remains a Mystery

One of the most human of all notions is the idea that some deserve more justice, more punishment than others. For instance, how many of us have felt that, while it was easy to forgive a son or a daughter, it is nearly impossible to forgive a parent. This is a perfect example of our struggle to be like God. The measure of grace that our good Father uses is applied equally to all. But when we mete out our application of grace, it's easy to assume that some deserve more "grace" than others.

Perhaps the simplest definition of Grace is - "**NOT** receiving what we deserve." Our problem with giving grace is that we bypass this definition for a more human application of justice. We want to know that "justice was served," and more often than not, our notion of "justice" is "served" up COLD.

Learning to have success through covenant will require a major shift in our character. We cannot understand a covenant with almighty God until we glimpse what it means to be a "giver" and not just a "taker."

To understand God is to know Him as good, as One whose very being IS LOVE. To understand Him is to want to be like Him. This is where we can break the very pattern of addiction at its core and root out the selfishness that feeds it!

A major step towards having a "Life Worth Living Sober" will come when we take ownership of the truth about ourselves. We will have to own the fact that if we want better outcomes we will have to make better CHOICES.

If I believe that God's forgiving grace is only something HE can do or that it's some kind of special attribute only for HIM, I miss the point. He doesn't just give us grace. He IS grace! And, He gives it and exhibits it with such love because He wants us to BE LIKE HIM.

A father finds no greater joy than to hear his child say, "I want to be like you daddy." And so it is with our Father

God, that nothing we can do will bring Him greater joy than to hear the cry of our hearts to be LIKE HIM.

As He is grace, so should we want to be grace to others. And, it is possible. By the Holy Spirit, Jesus has enabled us to become EVERYTHING HE IS!

When we choose judgment upon others rather than grace we are not being like our Father. We will have to learn how to "redeem" our bad situations the way God does, ... through love. We will have to stop reaching for "fig leaves" and covering things up rather than facing them.

Relational Faithfulness, the Foundation of Faith

As I purposely choose to make "sacrifices" in relationships, it will help me move away from the influence of demonic self-centeredness. Being a giver will open up my life to the influence of love and positive relationships.

One of the ways God teaches us to give is through the principle of the tithe. And, while nothing should ever take the place of the simple faith we have in Christ that connects us to God, you could say that tithing can work as a kind of "covenant connector" between us and God.

The tithe was never viewed by God as just a commandment to be kept, but as a partnership that allows us to engage in a covenant with Him. There were many examples of tithing in the Bible long before Moses laid it out as a commandment.

There was the "tenth" that Jacob promised to God at Bethel (Genesis 28:22); the tithe that Abraham paid to Melchizedek (Genesis 14:18-20); the tithe that Noah paid to God after the flood (Genesis 8:20); and even a tithe in the Garden of Eden in the form of a "tee" that God said was His. All these were set apart as belonging to God because of relationship rather than through a commandment.

To engage God in covenant means to connect with Him through the shared commitment and accountability of a covenant relationship. God wants us to form a bond with Him, to believe in Him, and to count on Him the way He believes in us. After all, His "gift" to us has been to suffer our shame, guilt, and punishment on the cross.

Our Father has shown that He believes in us so much that He would offer His Son to die in our place. What is a tenth of our worldly goods compared to that? Our part of the covenant commitment is the easy part!

When God says in Malachi 3:10, *"Bring all the tithes into the storehouse ... And try Me now in this... If I will not open for you the windows of heaven and pour out for you a blessing ..."* He is not making a demand. He is making a promise and an offer to engage with us in a covenant deal where we always come out the winner!

It is a plea for a committed engagement in relationship. He is saying, "just exercise your faith and faithfulness with Me and you will see that I am always FAITHFUL."

Covenant With God + Covenant With Others = Success

Another story in the life of David will tell us an awful lot about how and why he was so well-connected with God. It is the story of the covenant between Jonathan and David.

But, we need to pause for a moment and see that little David who killed the giant was already a giant of faith. The question is, how did he get there at such a young age?

What we find is that David lived a life of worship, devotion, and prayer. David had first developed his understanding of FAITHFULNESS in covenant while spending time with his father God out in the fields. The Bible tells us that he played a stringed instrument (something like a harp) and that he wrote great psalms or songs to the Lord.

David also wrote some of his prayers, as in the 23rd Psalm, "The Lord is my Shepherd ..." These songs and prayers were mostly a compilation of David's declarations about God. As he sang and worshipped, David had great revelations of God's nature and character. And as he meditated on Him, David knew Him, became like Him, and developed confidence in what the Lord's character could produce inside him.

Perhaps the greatest display of God's character in David's life was shown during a period when his mentor, King Saul, became tormented in his mind and wanted to kill David. It became a story about "winning" in relationships because David was a man filled with God's love and faithfulness.

Covenant Living - Never "Settles" for "Less"

On that same fateful day when David had taken the head of Goliath, he was taken to King Saul by Abner, the commander of the army. Saul inquired about David's father and his family, and the king's son was looking on. Saul's son, Jonathan saw in David a courage, an anointing and a presence of God that he could not help but admire. It made him want to be near David, to be like him and he immediately sought to make him his brother:

1 Samuel 18:1-4 - "... when (David) had finished speaking to Saul, the soul of Jonathan was knit to the soul of David ... Then Jonathan and David **made a covenant**, because (Jonathan) loved him as his own soul. And Jonathan took off the robe that was on him and gave it to David, with his armor, even to his sword and his bow and his belt."

Then, chapters 18-20 of 1 Samuel tell the story of madness and jealousy that came over King Saul against David. The King was so enraged in his jealousy that he even hurled a spear at his own son, Jonathan, when he perceived that he was siding with David. Saul clearly wanted to kill David, but because of a God-ordained covenant between

Jonathan and David, Jonathan took steps to protect David from his own father.

These two grown men, warriors of God's army, met in a field for one last time and wept as David sought a report from Jonathan about King Saul. Jonathan knew that David could never return to the king's palace because Saul was bent on killing David.

THIS is the picture of covenant relationship. This Jonathan, heir to the throne, was protecting the very man he knew was ordained to rule in his place. Because of **covenant**, he stood with a man of righteousness against the corruption of his own blood family.

Jonathan chose a righteous love forged in **Godly covenant** over the treasures and pleasures of this world. He chose David because he saw God at work and wanted nothing less than the abundant provisions of a God-blessed future!

David bowed down to Jonathan three times and they hugged and wept together for what would be the last time David would see Jonathan alive and … "Jonathan said to David, 'Go in peace, since we have both sworn in the name of the LORD, saying, 'May the LORD be between you and me, and between your descendants and my descendants, forever.'" (1 Samuel 20:42)

Learning to have success through Covenant will require that I learn how to live a God-focused life. It will take courage to make the tough choices that keep me on the path of God's presence and provision.

I will need to choose carefully and wisely whose "soul" I allow to be knitted together with mine. Making better choices will indeed lead to better outcomes in my life, but I will at times have to do battle with my own desires and appetites. Being content to choose the "narrow way" of the Lord will mean that I no longer allow myself to feel "entitled" to certain things.

But the winning will be sweet. It will be a great satisfaction for us just as it was for David.

David did become king of Israel. Much like you and I, he reigned as an overcomer through a life filled with trials and victories till his years were fulfilled in old age. Through covenant relationships with God and with countless others, David truly lived the Great Adventure of an Abundant Life.

It is said that in his last days King David wrote the following as some of his last words:

*"The Spirit of the LORD spoke by me, And His word was on my tongue. The God of Israel said, The Rock of Israel spoke to me: 'He who rules over men must be just, Ruling in the fear of God... He has made with me an everlasting **covenant**, Ordered*

in all things and secure. For this is all my salvation and all my desire; Will He not make it increase?"' (2 Samuel 23:2-5)

"Jesus said, ... Get a Life!"
"I have come that they may have life, and that they may have it more abundantly."
(John 10:10)

CHAPTER 6

Courage

Trying New Things Brings Change

It was cold in Chesapeake, Virginia during the winter of 1990. I remember it well because there were times that it was difficult to heat the old house where I volunteered as a mentor to recovering addicts. With my own addiction only five years in my rear-view mirror, I was now helping others and going back to school. Some days, I just really couldn't believe how drastically God had changed my life.

I had chosen a no-frills internship as part of my studies. I owed it to these men who struggled so much and had so much against them to be the one who loved and served them. I owed it because so many had made it their business to be there for me when I least deserved it.

It was a place called "Onesimus House," and I soon learned that these were the men no one else wanted. Most were two-or-three-strike losers who had come there on parole from prison. All of them struggled with addiction to drugs or alcohol and had come to Onesimus because they had little or no resources. Other programs just wouldn't take them.

One of my first assignments at Onesimus was to mentor a tough, jail-hardened man named Henry. Not knowing exactly what to make of me, he made it clear the first day that he was from the "hood" and that I just wouldn't understand. He was right and it didn't help that he was bit older than I was. I was still just in my twenties. He was kind enough to explain to me about "Onesimus" in the Bible.

Many weeks went by and, in time, I did manage to form a friendship with Henry. I was amazed at his love for the Bible and how he began to embrace dreams of becoming a "preacher." We would talk for hours about the Lord and how only His love can change a hard heart.

One day the following Spring, the time arrived when Henry was to graduate from Onesimus. My time with him had only involved the final months of his two years there and he was now eager to move on to face the world. It had become a powerful time of learning for both of us. An important part of my role was to help Henry prepare for transition to live back out on his own.

While I wasn't really a "novice" to this world of working with addicts, I was still terribly unprepared for what was about to take place.

I had worked at a Salvation Army Parolee Halfway House in downtown Dallas, Texas for a year before Onesimus. I had seen men fight and bleed and commit all manner of violations to get sent back to prison, often just because they couldn't hack it on the "outside." Some said they just wanted to go back because they at least knew they would get "three hots and a cot." Sometimes, we would lose men faster than they would come in, but none of that was able to prepare me for what was about to happen with Henry.

He taught me something so grave and profound that it is a lesson I will never forget. It was there in that testing place that I first understood how a lack of COURAGE can destroy a man's bright future even when he gets everything else right.

I was certain that Henry KNEW all about "triggers" to relapse and how certain people back in his home turf would most likely take him back to using. But, what I didn't understand was just how powerful familiarity can be.

When I read his after-care paperwork, I was in a panic. He was taking a job right back in his old neighborhood and had chosen an apartment about a block from his old home in the "hood." I asked him why he would do that and he just looked at me with those eyes that said, "You wouldn't understand" and shrugged his shoulders. I called in reinforcements one after the other to talk with Henry ... all the way up to the Director and all our discussions with him were to no avail. He was determined to go back!

He never told us why until his last day at Onesimus. Henry told one of the other men in the program that we just didn't understand and that he didn't know how to explain it. He said that he had always lived in that old neighborhood and didn't know anything else. His Mama was there. His Grandma was there and he thought he should be there to look out for his sisters who were still there too.

He had lived on that block and he had lived in prison but nowhere else. He was telling himself that he wanted to be a "light" back in that dark, dark place.

The problem was that Henry was not ready to be that "light," not yet anyway. We tried to encourage him to think of going back there some day when he was stronger. But his mind was made up. He took that job and he moved right back to what he knew. All of the Onesimus staff and volunteers had a bad feeling about this but we had to let him go.

A month or so after Henry moved out, I walked into Onesimus House one evening to a welcome of gloom and sorrow. Our Director was sitting with all the men in the living room in a big circle. It seemed that everyone there already knew something had happened to Henry and the Director was there to explain the details. He said, "I'm so sorry to have to let you all know that Henry passed away last night." He explained further that, "Henry died in a car wreck."

I later found out that Henry started drinking one night with several of those "crazy girls" from the "hood" he used to tell us about. All he had to do was let them in the door. It was the beginning of the end for Henry. Those girls knew how to push his buttons and they brought the alcohol. "Just a few drinks," he probably thought to himself. But his fate was sealed after the first drink.

When the whole story was finally told, it turned out that he was so ashamed about his relapse that he became severely depressed. He wouldn't talk to anyone who reached out to him, stayed drunk or high all the time, and pretended not to be home if anyone went by and knocked on the door.

The final act of this self-hating chapter in Henry's life was when he drove his car down a country road at over 100 miles per hour and veered off, slamming head-on into a tree.

The Police said the crash was intentional and his death was labeled a suicide. It wasn't pretty and the funeral was one of the most empty and disgusting moments of our lives.

In the weeks that followed, I found myself haunted by those words that came out of Henry's mouth. He had said, "I don't know nothin' else. My mama is there, my grandma is there, and my sisters…"

In the years that have passed since I met Henry, I've realized that Henry tried to do what countless others have tried to do and failed. HE TRIED TO GO BACK TO WHAT HE KNEW!

In our weak and illogical habit of fantasy-thinking, addicts are so often defeated right on the verge of victory when we are seduced by something "familiar." We settle for the comfort and security of a path of least resistance instead of the challenging and fruitful path God sets before us.

How many of us have to die? How many have to go back to prison before we learn that our deliverance is a battle to be fought, NOT some soft-landing into our comfort zone.

Henry died for one simple reason. He did not exercise "**the COURAGE to face the unfamiliar**."

During the months after Henry's death, those words from the Holy Spirit would swirl around in my head and would not leave me alone. I was marked for life by those thoughts because I was certain that Henry did not have to die.

It was NOT knowledge, support, tools or the cultivation of positive habits that Henry lacked. It was courage! And it is this same, specific courage that we will all need if we are to launch, unmoored to familiar things, out into the destiny God has for us. Real victory over the damage of addiction will not be had any other way.

We must launch out in faith with the "courage to face the unfamiliar" if we really want to live out this adventure called "Abundant Life."

Only those with Courage will make it Through the Wilderness

For people in Recovery, having a "life worth living sober" begins when we're ready to move beyond "recovery" in search of "abundant life." It always comes with a risk. All valuable things in life require taking a risk.

A "Life worth living sober" begins when we open ourselves enough to God's wisdom to enjoy a "recovery" that does not become a "wilderness experience." It comes when we have completely DECIDED that "settling" for less is NOT an option.

It happens when, come what may, we must cross the Jordon to lay hold of our inheritance. It happens because we have come to believe that God's plan for our lives is our *only* plan. Nothing else makes sense compared to trusting Him!

The "courage to face the unfamiliar" is never more clear than in the story of Joshua and Caleb and the Hebrew journey from Egypt to Canaan. These men had seen more of God's awesomeness than most of us would be able to stand. They had known the best and the worst of men and had determined to live their lives by one simple rule: *"Obey the Word of the Lord."*

Engulfed in the fear of spying out a strange land where cities and weapons were made of iron and where their champions were literal GIANTS, these men found courage when others shrank. They were but two among ten, rising against a tide of opposition that wailed in fear that they were *"grasshoppers in their own eyes"* (Num. 13:33, NIV).

It would take another 40 years, but these men of faith and courage were the only ones of that generation able to partake of the promise. From this story we gather that we should not think that the "timid" will posses the thing that God has promised. If we want to enter "abundance" in the Promised Land, we must always rise up in faith, hope, and in a measure of great *courage*.

Then, as if to put a fine tip on the point of the story, the Lord said to Joshua as he was about to enter Canaan: *"Be strong and* **courageous**. *Do not be afraid; do not be* **discouraged**, *for the* LORD *your God will be with you wherever you go."* (Joshua 1:9, NIV)

It was the "dis-courage-ment" they suffered in the wilderness that had risen time and again in their lives as the enemy of courage. It was the plague of "anti-courage" that had hounded them all those years through experiences of fear and unbelief. Now, with their eyes off the limits of their own pitiful resources and squarely upon the limitless capacity of God, they were ready. Strong and courageous, they could now cross over and posses the land!

What Makes One Person Able To "Overcome" While Another Remains a Cripple?

In the 1940's, during a time of great uncertainty and global instability, a notable author named Helen Keller penned these words, *"Avoiding danger is no safer in the long run than outright exposure. The fearful are caught as often as the bold. Faith alone defends. Life is either a daring adventure or nothing."*[1]

Keller was severely handicapped having been born deaf and mute and suffered what seemed insurmountable challenges. There was no known sign language or Braille or any such devices in those days to assist her with learning. But, with an insatiable hunger to know things and with the help of her teacher, Anne Sullivan, Helen Keller went on to write several books that became best sellers including, *Let Us Have Faith*, the book that contained the above quote.

We can see that faith, as defined by Helen Keller, is marked by an attitude of courage and an adventurous spirit. So, how does such a person, who, as a child was thought to be capable of only the most basic level of behaviors, become a best-selling author? What makes one person have the capacity to overcome such obstacles in life while another remains a cripple?

In her best-selling book, *Grit, The Power of Passion and Perseverance*, research Psychologist, Dr. Angela Duckworth, lays out a study of two traits that predict success and well-being. She calls them *grit* and *self-control*. The most interesting thing about Dr. Duckworth's work for Christians may well be the definitions she gives to these two traits.[2]

She defines *grit* as the "ability to sustain interest in and effort towards very long-term goals." And, she defines *self-control* as "the voluntary regulation of impulses in the presence of momentarily gratifying temptations." Isn't it interesting that these traits sound very much like things the Bible has been talking about for thousands of years.

Grit, as defined by Duckworth is actually very similar to an aspect of *faith* - "a sustained interest towards very long-term goals." And, *self-control* by her definition (impulse control in the presence of temptation) is very much like the *denial of self* that Jesus teaches when He tells us to take up our cross and follow Him (Luke 9:23, NIV).

The focus and tenacity of this *grit* is the mindset that separated Joshua and Caleb from the others. It is a kind of *grit* that must be woven into our faith so that it sustains us for the long haul. It is this *self-control* that will enable us to sustain our *courage* when we are tempted by our fears to throw in the towel.

These are the things that produce greatness in times of chaos and crisis and make overcomers of some while others fall into despair. It is Moses with the courage to face Pharaoh; it is Peter walking on the water while 11 disciples were still in the boat; it is Daniel staring down the lions and the 3 Hebrew boys dancing in the furnace. This is that which made Jesus set his face to go to Jerusalem when He knew they wanted to kill Him (Luke 9:51, NKJV). It is courage to beat the odds and a *courage to face the unfamiliar*.

When Problems Become Opportunities and Risk Becomes a Springboard

In the story about Henry and in my time at Onesimus, the lessons seemed hard and the truth felt cold. But what became important for me and for the other men in the program was something far beyond a grim and tragic loss. Henry's death became a story that opened a revelation. The Light of God began to shine on what we all needed to do.

As we were able to look beyond the bad decisions, the failure, and the loss, we felt something brighter begin to emerge. We had to choose. What would we take away from the experience? We could allow our disappointment and loss to cast doubt onto our faith or we could see it as an opportunity to dig deeper.

Knowing it was a failure of courage that killed Henry was not enough. God was after a better, more courageous response. If fear and a lack of courage had cost us our friend, what might it cost us if we did not turn this problem into our opportunity.

The way to ensure that Henry's death was not a waste would be for us to exercise courage in new ways. Our problems would now become our opportunities for courage and the risk we needed to take would become a springboard into our future!

CHANGE - all Courage Begins Here

If the definition of insanity is *doing the same thing over and over and expecting a different result*, then change and the courage to take risk can be the keys to a sound mind. It's not that all change brings progress, but that **all progress requires change**. We all get in a rut at times and it often requires courage and risk to break out into new personal growth.

There are times when doing almost ANYTHING different from your daily routine will actually be able to disrupt a spiral of depression. To stop getting what we've been getting, we may have to stop doing what we've been doing.

A healthy part of normal growth and development is for a person to be willing to try new things. For people in recovery, this can be really difficult. But the journey into abundant life requires that we take steps to break out of that small world our addiction has produced.

Change, Courage and a Faith That Requires Risk

If embracing change itself is a common act of courage, then saying YES to a journey into the unknown is often an act of transformational change. A step of faith into the unknown at the invitation of God ignites a revolutionary courage like nothing else can. It is an act of courage that always explodes into more growth and more courage.

Real faith takes courage because steadfast belief is willing to take action that often involves risk.

While some people are born with a more natural tendency to take risk, all believers can benefit from an occasional *roll of the dice*. Faith, we are told, is when we *believe* something strong enough that we are willing to take a risk to stand on that belief. Real faith comes with an expected end or promised outcome. It is not passive, but exercises a certain energy towards what is believed and expected.

Have you ever taken a certain job or moved to a certain place because you felt God was leading you? Have you been willing to go against your own natural inclinations and do something just because you felt the Holy Spirit nudged you in that direction? These are acts of faith that take courage.

Whenever we step up to the plate and swing hard at some curve ball God throws our way, we may absolutely believe we will knock it out of the park. But, deep down, we will know that we might strike out and miss that pitch entirely. This is what courageous faith looks like. It is not some formula and it is not guaranteed. An uncertain outcome is part of what makes it *faith* in the first place.

The Unknown Destination - Path to Abundant Life

The man we know as Abraham in the Bible is first introduced in Genesis, chapter 12, right after his father Terah has died. His name was still Abram when God starts to speak to him and this is the first thing God says, *"... Get out of your country, from your family and from your father's house, to a land that I will show you."* (Genesis 12:1)

God also made promises to Abram along with this call to journey into the unknown. God told him, *"I will make you a great nation; I will bless you and make your name great;... And I will curse him who curses you..."* (Genesis 12:2-3)

Abram took that first step of faith and he became Abraham, a man called the friend of God. It was Abram who the Bible says *believed God* when apparently no one else would and it was *accounted to him as righteousness.* (James 2:23)

Abraham became prosperous and enjoyed great benefits from his courageous steps of obedience. His life became an example of *the great adventure* that a life of courage before God was intended to be. It was full of risk and rewards and did not sink into the miry, stagnant living that marks so many. It was a life of abundance marked by great challenges that the man of faith would learn to overcome.

It Only "Works if You Work It"

Many who come to faith in Christ and who receive a great deliverance from addiction are not at first prepared for the battles that lie ahead. Just like the children of Israel who were delivered from the Egyptians, we may sense a great release from our bondage and great joy at the promise of a better life. We may enter into this new relationship with God feeling somewhat light-headed and almost giddy.

Yet, just like Abraham, Moses, Joshua and Caleb we soon come face to face with the necessity and real application of our faith. It is a spiritual principle set forth by God that applies to all faith journeys that **everything**

that has been promised must be possessed. To possess what God has promised will almost always require *courage*.

Joshua 23:5 says, *"And the LORD your God will expel them from before you and drive them out of your sight. So you shall **possess** their land, as the LORD your God **promised** you."* THIS was the moment for which they had wandered and waited 40 years for! What did God mean that they had to *possess* their land? Why wouldn't God remove the Canaanites and just make them disappear so Israel could just walk in and receive the land?

God had PROMISED the land, but now they had to POSSESS it! The very picture of how faith works, this story is there to teach us that we have a part to play. It means that God's promises are never meant to be some dream in a snow globe or a genie in a bottle that can be conjured up if we wish really hard. It tells us that faith operates as a contract with God that only *works if you work it* with real courage, fight, and persistence.

It's "the Unfamiliar" Because That's Where Courage Thrives

After learning a little of the cultures of most of the Caribbean Islands for a number of years, our Bible School had our first student from Guyana, South America. My wife, Ruth, and I were instructors and part of the administrative staff of

90

Caribbean Christ for the Nations in Jamaica and were always excited to meet new students. Desmond's arrival represented a breakthrough after one of our short-term missions teams had visited Guyana the previous summer.

He was a strong, determined young man who very quickly earned a reputation for his no-nonsense devotion to study and devout living. I was always amazed at the individual stories our students had to tell and Desmond was no exception. When he was close to finishing up his first year, I had an opportunity one day to ask him some questions about his life and about his journey. What he told me was an amazing illustration of how facing the unfamiliar can change a life forever.

Desmond was born into severe poverty in the ghettos of Georgetown. His mother had no education and he never had any real father figure. The men that were in his life growing up only abused and beat him on a regular basis. By the time Desmond was 14 years old, he was living homeless on the streets. He would have to do odd jobs, beg, and steal what he could just to survive.

One day Desmond was invited into a church and the people began to love him and demonstrated that they cared for him. Desmond was born again in that church and began to hang around it as much as he could. Some people in the church eventually took him in and, as his love for God grew, he became a youth leader in the church. One day the Pastor came to Desmond and asked if he would like to go to Bible college in Jamaica and said that the church would help pay for it if he would go.

The problem was that Desmond had never been anywhere except the Ghettos of Georgetown. When the Pastor told him that the school was in Jamaica, Desmond was overcome with fear. He said, "Isn't there a school here in Georgetown where I could go?" But the Pastor told him that our school had offered a partial scholarship and it was the only place he could afford.

Shaking in his boots, Desmond agreed to go and packed his bags to be off to Jamaica. He told me that when he first arrived, he didn't like the food and that he really felt out of place. When I asked him how he had overcome his fears and managed to do so well in his classes (he was an honor student with all A's and B's), he stopped and stared up at me with tears in his eyes and said, "Brother Fallin, you don't know the half of it. When I came hear, I didn't even know how to read!"

Desmond had been getting help from his dorm mates at night, but he also told me a marvelous thing about how he learned to read. He said that he told God that since he knew He wanted him to be able to read the Bible, he would believe God could teach him to read. He said, "Every time I would pick up my Bible I would pray, Lord, since you want me to be able to understand this book and preach to others, I'm trusting You to teach me to read!"

That young man not only overcame his fear of the unfamiliar, but with every step of faith, grew stronger and stronger. By his second term, he was not only reading, but became an "A" student in most of his classes. His story may not have been rags to riches, but it was a story of great courage and faith to face the unknown with God. Not only was he able to rise from a homeless life as a thief on the streets, but he became a great man of God and a preacher of the Gospel!

If *faith* is the *substance of things hoped for* (Hebrews 11:1), it means it works as a catalyst to literally bring things to pass. So, the *substance* of faith works with other things to create something new. And yet faith itself is made up of other *substances* that must work together for faith to exist.

Our first assumption about faith is that it consists of strong *belief* about something. Yet faith requires a *hope* and an *expectation* that produces action. In the Old Testament, during times when definitive action was needed, we find the phrase *be strong and of good courage* repeated 11 times. It has always been the failure to have COURAGE that has deprived us most when faced with a need for great *faith* to see things change.

"Jesus said, ... Get a Life!"
"I have come that they may have life, and that they may have it more abundantly."
(John 10:10)

CHAPTER 7

Purpose

God Has a "Blueprint" for my Life

Facing the VOID and Embracing the JOURNEY

The journey into abundant life can seem difficult to those who cannot see fruit in their labors when the road seems long and does not reach a desired end. Being able to survive a march to the promised land has always required great perseverance and a faith that can envision the other side.

So many in recovery go through periods of great temptation beset by overwhelming thoughts of giving up and going back to Egypt. These episodes are not a failure of discipline, a particular weakness, or any lack of effort in the person's life. They are most often the direct result of an emptiness and boredom caused by a great void. It is what's left whenever we cut off the flow of over-stimulating or mind-numbing substance abuse.

A very common complaint among addicts in recovery goes something like this: "I just don't know what to do with myself," or "I spent all my time either seeking to obtain drugs or doing drugs and now I just don't know what to do." At the core of this problem is a need to answer the question: "What do I do INSTEAD?"

What can fill this void? What could possibly take the place of the thrill-seeking, risk-taking lifestyle of getting high all the time? Sometimes, it is like going through a great period of grief after the death of a taunting lover.

From Meaningless to Faith-Filled Purpose

Once we have regained our courage and stepped into our own faith-filled journey, we need to aim our faith and courage towards something. What will be the object of my persistent courage? What is the prize that is worth living for or the outcome worth dying for?

I need to find my sense of purpose. A life worth living sober does not exist in the days of hapless self-indulgence. It can only be born out of the meaning that is gained through the pains of self-discovery. A life worth living sober involves having a revelation of why I am here. It must come as one of those "aha!" moments in life when a sudden rush of focus and joy tells me that this is what I was made for.

"Finding my Purpose is NOT so much a matter of finding the right thing to do as it is just doing the Next Right Thing!"

Unlikely Heroes - When Purpose Finds Me

In II Kings, chapters 6-7, the Bible tells the story of when the King of Syria laid siege upon Samaria. The city was in dire need and suffered a great famine. Chapter 7 begins with these words from the prophet Elisha, "Hear the word of the Lord ... Tomorrow about this time a seah of fine flour shall be sold for a shekel, and two seahs of barley for a shekel, at the gate of Samaria."

While the words of the prophet were met with disbelief, God was at work behind the scenes getting His most unlikely heroes ready to deliver some news that would rock the city. They were four lepers, sick, weak and suffering, who did not expect to live through the night. They did not have visions of doing anything great and certainly did not expect to be used by God to deliver the city by a great miracle.

They were sitting at the entrance of the city gate and began to speak frankly to one another: "Why are we sitting here until we die? If we say, 'We will enter the city,' the famine is in the city, and we shall die there. And if we sit here, we die also. Now therefore, come, let us surrender to the army of the Syrians. If they keep us alive, we shall live; and if they kill us, we shall only die." (II Kings 7:3-4)

They rose early and went down to the Syrian camp and were greatly surprised to find that no one was there. The Bible says that The Lord had caused the army of the Syrians to hear the noise of chariots and horses and, fearing they were being attacked, they got up and left everything behind in their haste. They left horses, tents, food, drink, clothing and even their gold.

So, those lepers began to help themselves. They ate, drank and carted off some of the treasure to hide it. But soon they were convicted saying to one another, "We are not doing right. This day is a day of good news, and we remain silent" (II Kings 7:9). So, they went and called to the gatekeepers of the city and told them what they found.

When the King of Samaria sent messengers to the Syrian camp they found it just as the lepers had told them and the people came out and began to plunder the tents of the Syrians. It was a miraculous deliverance and came about just as the prophet had said, "... a seah of fine flour was sold for a shekel, and two seahs of barley for a shekel, according to the word of the Lord." (II Kings 7:16)

Many of us have gone through the ravages of addiction and entered into recovery feeling sick, weak, and suffering a lot like those four lepers. Maybe we have felt that the world pushed us away and treated us like we were unclean just like they were. Still, the truth for us can be just like it was for them.

I may not look like I have much to offer. I may not look like I can do anything. But just like those lepers I may have to say, "What have I got to lose?" If four lepers on the verge of death could step out, take a risk, and save a city, how much more am I able to respond with what I have?

I cannot know how much my life will make a difference until I roll the dice and take a shot. Taking a healthy risk will sometimes bring about a miracle if I just dare to follow God's lead.

Four men found great purpose in their lives on a day when they least expected it. In a moment when they couldn't imagine their lives any worse, they were thrust into a plan from God that saved themselves and saved a city. They found purpose through a step of faith and their gift was to share with others.

The story is a rich example of God's wonderful *grace* and *mercy*. It helps us see that even when we struggle to find our purpose, we may sometimes see our purpose finding us as we choose to be faithful and obedient with God.

Finding Purpose: the Pivot Point for Abundant Life

Everything written in this book until now describes things that can help us step into the chapters that follow. It may seem like we're making no progress, but sometimes God is just moving us into a better position to receive what He has for us.

Picture a radical transformation or a miracle in your life as if it were a medical procedure and God is the Great Physician. When we go to a doctor, the first thing the doctor will do is examine the patient to see if he or she is a good candidate for the procedure. And so, with the Great Physician, we are more likely to receive from him the miraculous things we need if we make ourselves a ***good candidate*** in the first place.

I can only find my gifts and purpose and have deep satisfaction in my life when I am willing to go through God's radical transformation. It is a great life of fulfillment that will only come to those who are willing. If we want to find our purpose, we must embrace the journey and the encounters that God has planned for each one of us as an individual.

Fulfilling our Purpose Through Spiritual Gifting

The Bible tells us that King Saul was one day anointed by the Holy Spirit while walking among the prophets.

When he began to prophesy and act like the prophets, people looked at him and said, "Is Saul among the prophets?" (1 Samuel 10:11). This story plays out in a way that tells us that, while Saul was not actually a prophet, he was, however, set apart as one marked by God for an anointed purpose. Saul would be king and whether for good or for bad, he, himself would choose how his anointing would be used.

The first key to a fruitful exercise of spiritual gifts is to know that we are called and chosen by God. All Christian believers are called and chosen. The Bible refers to those who are with Him in Revelation 17:14 as called, chosen, and faithful. Still, we must all learn to step out by faith and walk out our calling to fulfill our destiny.

Just like our experience of purpose, spiritual gifts are sometimes confirmed in our lives when we suddenly experience that aha! moment. We suddenly realize, wow, I'm really good at this. People may tell us that we're good at something and it strengthens what God has already been stirring in our lives. No matter how it comes to us, we know that a giftedness is stirring when we experience great joy and motivation every time we do that certain thing.

It would make no sense to say that my gift is *serving* when, in reality, I find no joy in *serving*. The nature of a God-gift is that He will hardwire it into our souls to do that certain thing again and again. We will be consistently drawn to do it and motivated to learn more and get better.

Tempered by the Spirit

One of the ways we understand spiritual gifts is from the list Paul gave us in Romans, chapter twelve. This chapter has a list of seven gifts often referred to as *motivational gifts*. These gifts are described as tied to our own, personal design, built into the way God made us. If my Motivational Gift is *prophecy*, it is only natural to have motivations associated with *prophecy* such as wanting to *proclaim God's truth.*

Somewhat like personality, these gifts tend to bring with them certain common behaviors and tendencies. They may even have certain *rough edges* at first that have not yet been mastered through maturity. For instance, a person with the gift of *teaching* may at times be so caught up with *research* or *telling others* that they may find it difficult to be quiet and listen to what others have to say.

Even something profoundly God-given like a spiritual gift can, at times, be so humanly driven that it will chafe others in the way it is expressed. When we use our spiritual gifts, our relationships will often require some level of restraint as we learn what's appropriate in different situations.

We can be thankful that one of the works of the Holy Spirit is to help us *temper* our spiritual gifts. God loves us. And, it is so important to Him that our rough, immature edges are not so sharp that they push away everyone we meet.

A Process of Discovery - Trying Things for the First Time

It may seem strange, but many times people just stumble into their gifts and purpose by a seemingly random opportunity that presents itself. David probably had no idea what a great warrior he could become until he wandered upon a giant that needed to be killed! President George W. Bush had no intention of being a war-time president. He probably had no idea that he was to help develop a whole new concept for *homeland security* until those planes crashed into the Twin Towers on September 11, 2001.

This is one of the reasons that having courage to try new things is so important. We really don't know how good we could be at something until we try it for the first time.

A simple example of this is someone who has a great voice for singing. That person may never know they have a tremendous talent unless they first try to sing. My father and my brother both earned part of their living with their voices. But those tremendous voices might never have earned them a dime if they had never tried singing in the first place.

Sometimes, the gifting and purpose of something in our lives is actually revealed when we discover how much we love to do it. Cain and Abel probably exhibited gifts in their chosen vocation. Cain was a man who loved the soil but Abel was more inclined to shepherd the flock. Men and women are drawn into certain things because of a deep love and motivation that flows out of our gifts and purpose.

What a shame it would be to live out our lives frustrated and unfulfilled because we never tried things or never experienced anything that connected with our hearts' desire. This is why it's so important for us to try new things. A thrill never experienced will never be a thing we love. A food never tasted cannot become one of our favorite things to eat!

What if some of the great people in history never tried a certain thing for the first time? What if King David never played the liar or never held a sword. What if Samson never even discovered that he had great strength; or what if Moses never saw his first miracle because he was afraid to try? What if Thomas Edison never did a second scientific experiment just because he had failed in the first?

The great Olympic swimmer, Michael Phelps, is known as the most successful and most decorated Olympian of all time, with a total of 28 medals. He also holds the all-time record for Olympic gold medals. Phelps began swimming at the age of seven and is often quoted as saying, "The only reason I ever got in the water was my mom wanted me to just learn how to swim." So, what would Michael Phelps have become if he had never even tried to swim for the first time?

Looking Within - the Purpose Is in the Design

Knowing a clear sense of PURPOSE is often more of a journey than it is a destination. What we do know about our purpose in one season may not remain the same in a different season of our lives. What is confirmed as a focus of our energies and talents now may later take a back seat to something more important. When God is causing us to grow, we may see the *priorities* within our purpose tend to shift and transition.

Our conviction, level of passion, and our ability to function may all be factors that affect how a clear purpose begins to emerge. We all know people who regularly express their frustration and dissatisfaction with life. We may hear them say, "I just don't know what I'm supposed to be doing." They may complain that they hate their job, or talk about how boring it is to go to work everyday. These may be normal experiences to have on the one hand, but it may also be a sign that something is badly misaligned in their life.

A sense of satisfaction, contentment, and generally feeling that life is as it should be is a wonderful byproduct of living a well-balanced life. In the same way, purpose is not so much a thing to be "found," as it is something that emerges from within when my life is well-aligned with God. When we say that God has a *purpose* for my life, it is not some external idea that has to be coaxed out of the mind of God. My Purpose is already a built-in part of me by God's design.

God's purpose is something woven deep into the fabric of my soul. It should easily rise to the surface just like a fingernail knows it belongs on my finger, or a hair knows to grow on my head. It is embedded as though it were part of my DNA.

People waste years just waiting on a sign or a message from God about their purpose. They have a contrived image in their minds that their purpose must come by way of special revelation from God when, in reality, it will only be revealed by way of special expression of themselves.

We may be waiting for Him to reveal it while He is waiting for us to move into alignment and be *tuned in* to how He made us. It is like a song we were born to sing. It's like the 1924 Olympic runner, Eric Liddell, in the movie, "Chariots of Fire" when he said, "*When I run, I* **feel His** *pleasure!*"

Clarity about my purpose is always like that. We will know it when we "*feel His pleasure.*" It isn't often that people have some grand prophetic experience or message from God as the way that they discover their purpose. In fact, it is more often in one of life's simpler moments that suddenly the shear joy in a certain thing makes it clear that THIS is what I was made for. I may even say to myself, "THIS is my thing and I know it because it makes my heart sing. I can feel the joy of God's heart."

Quiet, Balance, & Alignment - the Atmosphere for Purpose

In this way our gifts and calling can emerge for us in that place of balance, alignment and being in tune with God. The answer to who and what we were meant to be can easily become clear in a quiet and intimate place with ourselves and God. It is better this way because many have had their hearts and ambitions misdirected through the misguided efforts of people with good intentions.

It's better to have God call forth His will directly than to depend on others to speak for God. Too many *mama-called preachers* have ended up on the dust pile of ministry because they were not listening for God's song in their own hearts.

Breaking Out of Survival Mode: the Keys - Gifts and Purpose

Once we come into alignment with God's purpose from within, there is one other question that every Christian should ask themselves: "What was I *born again* for?" It is a simple question, but it is profound because most don't ever ask it.

It is also one of those questions that anyone coming out of addiction should never fail to ask! If the only real, permanent way out of addiction is to be *born again* in Christ, then understanding what I'm supposed to do with my new, *born-again* life becomes a critical question to answer.

When the destructive power of addiction has taken its toll, many who manage to get sober find it difficult to aspire to anything new. Our motivation to have goals may be minimized and the idea of being *ambitious* isn't even on the radar. Most addicts who come into recovery are *stuck* in a *survival mode* and find it difficult to live any other way.

But, when it comes to having *breakthrough*, we have a powerful, God-given weapon that can blow *survival mode* right out of the water. It's called ***The Holy Spirit***! This weapon is little known and not well understood because too many Christians don't *know* the Holy Spirit and what He wants to do for them.

One of the greatest things God did through Jesus Christ was to send the Holy Spirit as a *Helper, Counselor, and Friend*. The Holy Spirit is the power and the presence of God that is with us and is always available to us right NOW!

If I say, "I see the Holy Spirit working in your life to develop a gift of teaching or an artistic ability," that specific guidance may move someone to draw help from the Holy Spirit so they can grow and develop. With the ever-present help of God's Spirit in our lives, we're never alone or without help to face the challenges of healing and change. This is so important because the Holy Spirit is a *person* we can talk to at any time and any place.

It is true that anyone who has experienced a broken and devastated life knows that hopeless feeling we feel when trying to see things change. Yet, we can always feel more confident about new challenges and accomplishments when we know we have the ever-present help of the Holy Spirit.

The beautiful thing is that the Holy Spirit is often at work in our lives clarifying our Spiritual Gifts and Purpose. Without the Spirit's help, many remain trapped, trying to make sense out of their life. But when we invite the Holy Spirit to be our active partner, we find He is always faithful, revealing things and empowering us to carry them out.

Discovering our *gifts* and *purpose* and fulfilling our *destiny* will lead us to what Jesus meant by "Abundant Life." And, while it can be sad to leave others behind, trapped in the wilderness of *recovery*; we will find joy in knowing that our own lives have become an example of what is possible with God's help. Finding our own *gifts* and *purpose* and learning to live life to its fullest can be a huge step towards having a *life worth living sober*.

"Jesus said, ... Get a Life!"
*"I have come that they may have life, and that
they may have it more abundantly."*
(John 10:10)

CHAPTER 8

Satisfaction

Satisfying Occupation & What To Do Instead

I remember one time, I was just sitting there, flipping through channels and watching the news. I heard the News announcer say something that struck me as very telling and sickening to think about. He said that a recent survey indicated that 70% of Americans actually hated their jobs.

I don't know about you, but that hit me like a ton of bricks. It felt like it was a commentary intended just for me. It was a moment that only happens when you hear something that rings so true that it's like a slap in the face! It can shake you to the core.

I don't recall feeling like I actually hated my job, but I knew that at times it made me miserable. It was a thought that affected me in a profound way and I made up my mind right there that I wanted to find a job that I enjoyed.

Sometimes we have a rush of insight like this and we just know that it comes from God. That moment was very much like that for me and it was as if God had said to me, "Steve, you won't make it if you don't find a better way to be more satisfied with your life." It was true for me like it's probably true for many others reading this that have faced this struggle. The problem is "boredom" and it is a powerful trigger for substance abuse and addiction for millions of people.

I knew that I was deeply dissatisfied with a lot of things. It wasn't anybody else's fault and it wasn't because people in my life were failing me terribly. It wasn't even that I had made terrible choices and gotten myself into some horrible commitment I couldn't keep.

I was dissatisfied with my life because I hadn't done very much to go after the things that would bring me satisfaction. My approach to life at that point had always been—"just take it as it comes." "Que Sera Sera, whatever will be will be." That was me. No one had ever told me that you only get what you want in life when you make up your mind to go after it.

My life wasn't being lived in an intentional way at all. Up to this point in my life, I had pretty much just taken whatever life brought my way and tried to make the best of it. I made a decision that day and it was a decision that caused things to begin to change. I decided that instead of letting life have an impact on me, I would begin to live each day making the effort to have an impact on life!

Satisfaction and Fruit That Remains

That decision to be intentional is only one part of an equation that can bring us satisfaction in our lives and in our work. It's an important part, but won't produce results unless paired with a big dose of *self-discovery*. Satisfaction and fulfillment only come to those who actually *discover* something they are gifted to do and then *go after it*.

In Deuteronomy 35:30-33, the Bible describes something really special along the journey of the children of Israel. God was helping the Israelites grow in their relationship with Him as He gave them instruction on the Tabernacle and the ways of worship.

The people had responded to God with lavish gifts of material for the Tabernacle and God was showing Moses how to use what had been given. Then Moses describes how God would choose some of them to do special work because He had made them *gifted* to do certain things:

*"Then Moses said to the Israelites, 'See, the LORD has **chosen** Bezalel son of Uri, the son of*

113

*Hur, of the tribe of Judah, and he has **filled him with the Spirit** of God, with **wisdom**, with **understanding**, with **knowledge** and with all kinds of **skills** — **to make** artistic designs **for work** in gold, silver and bronze, **to cut and set** stones, **to work** in wood and **to engage in all kinds of artistic crafts.**'" (Deuteronomy 35:30-33)*

These verses establish an important Biblical *principle.* The Bible is telling us God chooses people for specific kinds of VOCATION in life and gives them gifts and talents to excel in it. It is saying that (at the very least) we can look to God and to His Spirit for wisdom, understanding and knowledge about how to do specific kinds of work.

So many go through life without ever looking for what God has put in them to make them excel in a specific job or line of work. But why would it seem strange to go to our Maker to ask Him what He made us to do? This is a simple, but very profound question. What was I born to do? Did God create me with abilities for a specific kind of work?

So often we just think that God has *purpose* and *calling* for Pastors or Missionaries or those who go into full-time ministry. But does God also have a purpose for the butcher, the baker, and the candle-stick maker?

Can a factory worker find just as much satisfaction in his work as an artist who creates beautiful paintings? He or she CAN if that work is something done in the fullness of God's Spirit. Nothing is more satisfying than our accomplishments done with all the skill that comes from the enabling power of God's grace!

SATISFACTION with life doesn't have to be a fleeting emotion that comes and goes like the wind. It isn't based on whether we've had a good day or a bad day. To be truly *satisfied* with my life and my work means that I am living in an alignment with God's plan and destiny in a way that produces **FRUIT**.

Real satisfaction has never been about wealth or fame or who dies with the most "toys." It is measured by the integrity that makes a man keep his word and stay true to his commitments. It is known by that relaxing breath that comes with a *job well done*.

Godly satisfaction is work that feels *full* toward the end of our days because we've done our best and left our mark. We first begin to know satisfying work and a satisfying life because of fruit that will remain to form a lasting legacy.

The "School of Hard-Knocks" and Learning To Listen

If you grew up like me, you know what it's like to waste your youth by not really *listening* to anyone. I was a terrible listener as a young man and, looking back, I believe it cost me dearly.

I didn't listen to parents. I didn't listen to teachers (at least, no more that I *had to*). I didn't even know how to listen to the world and life around me as it tried to tell me things. Indeed, the world around me was trying to tell me really important things about myself that I needed to hear.

The *school of hard-knocks* is not really a place for good listeners. But it is very much the schoolhouse designed for hard-headed, non-listeners like myself. The funny thing is so many of us end up fully registered as a student in the *school of hard-knocks* without ever even realizing we're on our way there.

Once you arrive in class, you remember hearing people say that if you would LISTEN, you wouldn't have to make the same mistakes they made. But now you know that you are where you are in the *school of hard-knocks* precisely because you DIDN'T LISTEN. Now, all you want to know is what you have to do to get out of this place!

The fact that we all understand what we mean by this *school of hard-knocks* is itself an indication that LIFE is always trying to *teach* us something. We all know that life does not take NO for an answer.

Life as a *teacher* can sound kind of like a benevolent Mafia Boss. The *teacher* usually begins each lesson by saying, *"Now, we can do this the easy way, or we can do this the hard way. But, we gotta do this."*

Even though we know that *Life* is going to teach us a lesson, it's still so easy to miss what it's trying tell us. It's mainly because we're just not paying attention. We may have the skill of *song writing, fixing things,* or great *artistic design* locked inside, but never it never gets expressed. Being out of step with *Life* has consequences and some opportunities may be lost forever simply because we didn't see it and just walked right on by.

Our greatest capabilities may never become real simply because we don't see it, hear it, or believe it. We may have potential to be the best mechanic or the best builder in town. But we won't be when we have missed our cues to excel in it because we didn't hear the affirmation when it came.

While there are many things in life that can deafen our ears or quench our fire to be the best, we cannot let that stop us from tuning in. We could all look back and think to ourselves, "I could have been the best or really excelled if it hadn't been for _____," — just fill in the blank.

But, whatever may have stood in my way, whether discouraging words, lack of resources or a major crisis, what matters is if I overcome it. I can continue to believe a lie about myself or agree with God that I am *fearfully and wonderfully made.*

Whatever I choose to believe, it's important to realize that I won't develop my God-given skills until I begin to recognize them and cultivate them. I alone am responsible for what I choose to do with my life and no one else will have to answer for it.

If I make a quality decision to *listen* for what life is trying to tell me and if I will tune in to the Holy Spirit and line up with what He is saying, my potential can still be unlocked and unleashed. Finding a satisfying occupation may not be as hard as I thought if I will let life tell me what I am good at and go after it!

Created to Enjoy "Work"... And "Work" To Be Creative

Committing ourselves to *work* is a Godly attribute since God Himself is a worker. In Genesis 2:2, the Bible says:

*"And on the seventh day God ended His **work** which He had done, and He rested on the seventh day from all His **work** ..."*

So, created in the image of God, Man also was designed to be a worker. In fact, it is difficult to really be "like" God unless we are willing to give ourselves to "*work*." Like God, we are able to be very "*creative*" in our work and bring things into being out of our *mind's eye* or imagination.

Everything God created was "*good*" and He has made us also capable of bringing forth "*good*" things into the earth. If, on the other hand, I allow myself use the work of my hands to bring forth things that are evil, I am nothing like my Father, God. In order to be truly satisfying, my work must bring forth "Fruit" or "Fruitfulness" in my Father's eyes.

Just like our Father, we have been made to "create" and produce in our environment in ways that will make new and make better the things we touch. We have been designed so that our influence upon every new thing we find should bring improvement and leave it better than it was when we found it.

The image of God is still stamped at the core of every human being so that even our words should influence the things around us for the better. God spoke and it was so and it was good. And so it should be with us that our presence and our touch upon the earth should produce something good. The Divine Intent for the creation of man has always been for our lives to be a creative expression of who God is.

Five Arenas of Work - our God-Given Design for Work

In Genesis 1:28, the Bible says:

*"Then God blessed them, and God said to them, 'Be **fruitful** and **multiply; fill** the earth and **subdue** it; **have dominion** over ..... every living thing that moves on the earth.'"*

Our God set forth His example as our role model for work; but He also gave us a clear and simple *"blueprint"* for the satisfying work of man.

Verse 28 of Genesis 1 lays out a set of **5 distinct categories** of work that are to be the arenas for Man's purpose and destiny. Some of us will excel in one or perhaps two of these arenas. Others may be capable of working in all 5, but all of us are able to find satisfaction in at least one of the good areas of work that God has assigned to mankind.

Not intending to give an exhaustive explanation of these categories of work, a short summary can be useful in the way we think about fulfillment in work. Right after God said that He created Man in His own image (Genesis 1:26 & 27), the Bible immediately lays out these 5 expressions of work that are given for man. In other words, these are given to man as a way to express the image of God in ourselves because in doing them we are being most like God.

Work that is carried out in the way we are designed (in the image of God) will always be the work that will bring us fulfillment. No man or woman will ever be more fulfilled in their work than when it is done as an expression of the God-image inside.

Perhaps you will see yourself and something about the way you are designed as you read through some of these descriptions of work. If you do, it may well be a witness of the Holy Spirit inside letting you know that is one of the things you were designed to do.

__Be Fruitful:__ meaning - Something is fruitful when it multiplies or adds to what's already there - producing more of something.

The "Be Fruitful" arena of work is probably the area that almost everyone fits into one way or another. Work that is "fruitful" can be anything that *"adds value," "produces,"* or *"sows seeds"* into the lives of others.

Some of the occupations that clearly work done in spirit of being fruitful can include any kind of work that makes things. It can be a *craft* or a skill that *constructs* or *builds* things. It can be in some form of farming or manufacturing and is involved anytime that production of something is the main outcome of the work.

Workers who spend most of their time in the business of producing should seek the Lord for wisdom and grace to find fulfillment and satisfaction in the quality of what they produce. A fruitful occupation can be a very satisfying occupation because it usually results in something very tangible that can be looked at as the *"fruit"* of ones labor.

__Multiply:__ meaning - Something multiplies when it increases or expands greatly - to grow in number.

The "Multiply" arena of work is something that many of us do either in our work or in some way for a cause that we care about in our "community." Causing things to increase in number is a very important skill that is in demand across many areas of society. For instance *"Campaign Managers"* are great "multipliers" in politics because of their skill in multiplying the number of people voting for a particular candidate.

Reproducing children is perhaps the most common way that humans multiply and *Parenting* is a further way that Moms and Dads reproduce themselves in their children. *Teachers, Trainers, Mentors* and *Activists* are all in the business of multiplying the number of people who know things, have skills or have understanding about certain subjects.

In Christianity and the Church, Evangelists are a great example of work that involves multiplication because the goal of Evangelism is to increase the number of Believers. A multiplying occupation is satisfying to many people because they get to pour their knowledge, wisdom or skills into someone else. We can probably all be multipliers in one way or another.

Fill: *meaning - to make "full," add value or beauty, or meet a want or need.*

The "Fill" arena of work includes all the ways that the works and services of others make our lives "full." This can mean that they add to our lives with some form of *"service work"* or they many provide something "new" that we didn't have before.

"Creative Designers" are particularly the kind of workers that are constantly filling our lives with new beauty and creative ideas. But there are many other "Fillers" in the world that regularly add to what we have by *"innovations,"* *"new inventions,"* *"creative arts"* or *"technology."* Some are actively working with God to *"Fill"* the earth through the creation of new *"music,"* *"media"* or other form of enjoyment that makes our lives "full."

A "filling" occupation can be very satisfying because it always involves some form of "giving" into the lives of others. "Fillers" may even be involved in "sales" in the sense that they bring new products into our lives. "Filling" the earth in obedience to the command of God can be very fulfilling work when the spirit is motivating us to be someone that adds to the lives of others.

Subdue: *meaning - to hold down, put back or defeat - to bring low or calm down.*

The "Subdue" arena of work is where the outcome of work brings control, order or good management into play.

Most of the work done in this arena involves taming something or keeping under control so that it doesn't get out of line. All forms of *"risk management"* such as *"Insurance," "Healthcare"* and *"Accounting"* fit into this category as well.

Great *"administrators," "managers," "government workers"* all fit into this arena because they all keep something or someone in line or at bay in order to maintain order in our world. Those who work to maintain "security" in various environments as we go about our day to day affairs are also in the work of "subduing" potential threats that could disrupt our lives.

Occupations that *"subdue"* the many threats and forms of volatility that interrupt our lives are vital to our ability to function. Even "counselors," and "therapists" are those who help us "subdue" things that could pose a threat to our daily lives. These workers not only help us maintain order but they help us keep our peace in a world that presents many things that can easily get out of control.

Have Dominion: *meaning - To have charge of or rule over - to control an area or territory and have power through legal authority.*

The "Have Dominion" arena of work involves workers who enforce authority or rule over something. They may also be *"explorers," "conquerors,"* or those who bring a territory into submission. *"Police"* officers, *"soldiers"* in the military and *"first responders"* are all good examples of those whose work requires them to "have dominion" over something.

Work that helps us have dominion is important because God gave authority over the earth to Man. Satan, the greatest threat to all mankind, was already there in the Garden of Eden when the first Man arrived. It was because Adam was given this charge, "Have Dominion" and failed that we live in a "fallen world" in the first place. Having dominion is always involved in the work of our top leaders such as a *"president,"* *"CEO,"* or *"executive director."*

Occupations that do the work of "having dominion" often hold our highest admiration because they include champions like our star "athletes" (modern-day gladiators) and the "astronauts" of our space industry. And yet, day to day workers in such things as the "transportation industry" are a vital way that increases our "dominion" over the earth as they help us expand our access to places we could not go before.

As Christians, we can all take part in an important aspect of having dominion when we serve in the work of The Kingdom of God. We can help extend and expand the dominion of God's kingdom in the earth as spread the Light of God's Love in ways that expose and expel the darkness. God's will for Man has always been that we give ourselves to the WORK that ensures His dominion over all the earth!

Having a "Mind To Work" and Enjoying It!

There's a verse in the Bible that demonstrates the great impact that we can have when we are committed to accomplish something through the God-given purpose of work. In Nehemiah 4:6, the Bible says:

*"So we built the wall, and the entire wall was joined together up to half its height, for the people **had a mind to work.**"*

The book of Nehemiah is a story of a miraculous turnaround in an impossible situation. Under Nehemiah's direction and inspiration, they were able to build the wall at a miraculous pace that was considered impossible to do. A wall that had been in disrepair for decades was suddenly raised almost overnight because the *"people had a mind to work."*

Having a mind to "work" goes a long way when it comes to finding a "satisfying occupation." And while enjoying our work isn't going to be some kind "cure" for addiction or anything else in a person's life, it is a huge part of having "abundant life" the way that Jesus wants us to. So many people have found sobriety only to lose it again because they did not get intentional about how they "occupy" their time.

When we are intentional about finding the right work, we can go on a journey of "self-discovery" with God and seek Him to get us plugged into just the right job. The kind of work we do can be anything as long as it's in alignment with God's design and purpose for my life so that God's will for me can be fulfilled. It's not mysterious and it's not some tricky spiritual revelation that we have to have in order to have God's best.

Having a satisfying occupation and finding joy and fulfillment in work is not that hard as long as I am willing to get to know God and seek His help to get to know myself. Work was created by God and should be done through the Spirit of God as part of the nature of God working in us.

King Solomon once said work should be something we enjoy: - Ecclesiates 3:22 "... *there is nothing better for a person than to* **enjoy their work**, ..."

"Jesus said, ... Get a Life!"
"I have come that they may have life, and that
they may have it more abundantly."
(John 10:10)

CHAPTER 9

Healing

Making Room for Others

Opening Up - From Smallness to Abundant Life

Traveling this journey of rebuilding our lives will eventually cause us all to arrive at the same place. It is a place that presents us with the ultimate challenge— *rebuilding our relationships*! No other aspect of our lives suffers more damage or lies in greater ruin from the ravages of addiction.

No other kind of restoration makes us work so hard. But it will be worth it because no other part of Abundant Life reaps such great rewards as rebuilding healthy relationships.

Making room for others is the greatest challenge on the journey to rebuild because it will cost us the roots of our selfishness. Thinking back to the beginning of this road to a *Life Worth Living Sober*, we talked about "*moving beyond the traps of addiction AND recovery.*" We talked about "*the way The Holy Spirit can move us from that small, self-*

centered life to a Life full of His Presence and fruitful relationships."

We will have to be HONEST about the damage, honest about our selfishness, and truly honest about the way we hurt others before the relational "rebuilding" can begin.

Our life in Addiction becomes so *"small"* because the very nature of Addiction is to be consumed with nothing but "Self." We eventually become obsessed with the pains, comforts, and experiences of "Self" and nothing else.

When we become fully trained in the devilish arts of loving "things" and using people and when we have totally used all our relational "credit" and burned all our bridges, the ravages of addiction are almost complete. Then, finally, when our "consumption" of people is turned on ourselves because no one else is left, that's when we discover just how "small" our world can become.

But this brokenness is always the place where real healing can begin *if we let it.* Our "smallness" in that brokenness will actually be a good thing *if we let it.*

You might say, as horrible as it may sound, that it is "good" that our lives became so small and broken. It was out of "Love" that God allowed it. If it didn't kill us but brought us to a place where we could be humble and teachable, we should consider ourselves most fortunate.

In this small and broken condition we may be able to find hope and learn to appreciate the "relationships" God gives us again. Out of our new-found gratitude for others, we may be able to "enlarge" our lives and make room for love, life, and true fulfillment.

This part of our transformation and rebuilding may take longer and will require us to work a little harder. It is stepping into the deeper wells of "Abundant Life." It is deeper because it reaches into our inner, private world.

It may require the tearing down of walls, the renunciation of lies we've believed, and an opening of our hearts to inner healing. The healing of relationships requires that we must have a healing of our Soul.

It will take courage and a willingness to knock off the scabs of our old wounds, but the exposure of those things will be good. The Sonlight of God's love will bring deep healing to the root issues of our lives if we stay willing to FINISH the Journey!

Relationships & What Happened Way Back When

In the Fall of 1965, my family suffered a series of events that would leave an indelible mark on everything that followed. I will never forget one particular day in that season of our lives. It is etched into my memory like nothing else I remember experiencing as a child. I had not seen my mother for several days, but I had no idea that the mother I had known since my birth would never come home the same.

It was just before my 6th birthday and my life as a child was in a burst of constant learning. I wanted to know everything and my parents were just getting used to having one of those children who never stopped asking questions—24 hours a day.

But on that day, I was in turmoil, forced to think about things and ask questions that a five-year-old shouldn't have to ponder. It was the day that we buried my little sister, Amelia Ann because she had died shortly after birth a few days before.

I remember being in the car with my brother and my father. Our dad drove that 30-mile trek to the cemetery in Macon like he was in a trance. He wasn't singing or whistling or doing any of the normally cheerful things my father was known to do. The silence was deafening and, in my little mind, this dreaded journey seemed like it would take an eternity.

I pressed my father for answers that day, right there in that car. I remember knowing that he was hurting because of his silence but how patient he was with me when I insisted on answers to my questions.

At five years old, I demanded to know how this could happen. I insisted on him telling me how babies were made, what happened when they were born, and how, after only two hours of life, my little sister was about to be buried in the ground.

When I look back on it, I feel immensely grateful that my father was willing to patiently answer my questions. And when I think of that day in light of all the details that were later told to me by my mother, I can't imagine just how hard that must have been.

There were so many things going through my little mind that I couldn't comprehend as a child. Very often, when a traumatic experience effects the life of a child, it is the overload of events in the lives of adults that makes it so bad. Multiple, simultaneous events like this had so effected my mother that she was hurled down into deep depression. She wasn't with us in that car because she couldn't be. She was heavily sedated.

When she did come home after the funeral, my mother's ability to show affection to the family was almost non-existent. She'd had a complete mental and emotional breakdown.

It took years of deep inner healing and reflection before I realized that in my little five-year-old mind it was as if I had lost my baby sister and my mother in the same day. To me, the mother I had known, the one that went to the hospital to have a baby, simply never came home.

It was only after several deep, personal conversations in the final months of my mother's life that I ever learned what had affected her so much. My mom and I had been terribly alienated because of my reactions to her as a teenager. While she was struggling to cope, her depression would sometimes manifest in fits of rage. My reaction was always to fight back and rebel against her authority.

I loved my mother deeply; but in an effort to share this story openly and truthfully as an illustration of the things that happen in families, I need to share some unpleasant things. My mother and I both became addicted to drugs.

By the time I was 14 years old, my choices led me down a path filled with all kinds of illegal drugs and alcohol use. Mom was addicted to Valium and other prescription drugs and the battle was on. Honestly, if you could have seen us, you would have thought we must have been competing to see who could act the craziest!

In those last months of her life, Mom fought a brave battle with terminal cancer. When she knew she was dying she asked me to sit and talk with her on multiple occasions. She would tell me stories I had never heard about the family and wanted me to know the truth about a lot of things I had never been told.

She wanted me to understand what happened to her and one day she shared the whole story. She told me how she had buried her father just three months before my baby sister had died and she explained to me how that had affected her emotionally.

Then, as she pulled an old letter from a bedroom drawer, she said, "I need to show you something that I've never told you about." It was a letter from a woman apologizing to my mother for seducing my father.

There I was, nearly 50 years old and weeping with overwhelming empathy for a woman I had despised most of my life. What overwhelmed me most was that she told me she had received this letter about my father's moral failure about a month before Amelia Ann died.

"It was all just too much," she said. My mother sat there and explained that she knew it had changed her when the baby died. She said she was sorry about the angry person she had become. It was the best reconciliation I have ever known and I will always be grateful for those last moments I shared with her.

Childhood and the Experience of Trauma

When we are honest about it, most of us can look back on our experiences and see how broken relationships seem to always go hand in hand with addiction. It all becomes a vicious cycle as broken relationships produce addiction and addiction produces more broken relationships.

The purpose of telling this story is to create a context for asking some important questions: How many of us have left a trail of broken relationships in our wake because of childhood trauma that led us to some false conclusions? What lies have we believed because we felt unloved or abandoned by someone? What inner vows have we made because of fears and false beliefs?

The kind of trauma that triggers an intense reaction in one child may not produce the same reaction in another. This is true even among children who grow up together in the same household. The measure of the impact of trauma on a child is not just the intensity of the experience; but it is also greatly affected by how the child perceives the intensity and the atmosphere around the child at the time.

Abundant Life Is for Overcomers Who Won't Settle for Less

This chapter is written as a challenge to those in recovery who so often *settle* for less than the *best*. It is about overcoming the barriers that have kept us from enlarging our inner world and making room for others. It is a line, drawn in the sand, where someone says to you, "there really is **MORE**, and I dare you to go after it!"

We need to talk about taking the required risk to be able to grow and learn to **love** again. We need to talk about how we can build the foundation that makes healthy relationships possible. Some of us will need to take a long, hard look at how we can come to know that we are Truly Loved by God!

It's true that our lives are shaped by the things that happened to us as children, but let us remember that we are called *Overcomers* in the Bible because *overcoming* is possible! These faulty roots from our childhood can and should be dealt with in our transformation process, but they are NOT *excuses* to stop trying, fighting, loving and living.

Thank God He has given us a method for rebuilding our very *thoughts*, *patterns*, *feelings* and *attitudes*. It is that normal Christian process we refer to as the *renewing of the mind* (Romans 12:2).

Relational Healing & the Flow of God's Love

If we don't know anything else about God, most of us have known THIS since our childhood: "For God so LOVED the world that He GAVE..." (John 3:16).

We may miss the most important point of this verse, however, if our attention is drawn to the *sacrifice* and we don't see that it was done out of LOVE. This verse tells us some very important things about God that we may desperately need to know. It tells us that He is a LOVER and a GIVER.

We could study and know all the Theology there is to know and still not benefit much from it if we never discover how to step into the flow of God's *love*! It was out of LOVE that God created Man and placed him in a garden with divine order, boundaries, and everything good.

It was Love that compelled God to create a *helper* and *companion* for Adam so that he would not be alone. And, it was Love that moved God to give Man a CHOICE.

The Lord God had created an earth with design, rules and *truth* that Man could live by or Man could choose to go his own way and break the relationship. It was because ***love*** does not control and does not manipulate or dominate that God allowed the man to have Freedom to walk away.

It was also *love* that made a WAY for Man to come home and find reconciliation. It was this *love* that the Man was created for, to both receive and give away.

Being created in the *image of God*, all human-kind has been designed to be both recipients and channels of God's LOVE in the earth. No other purpose and no other destiny for our lives can be greater than our role as *carriers* of God's LOVE.

It is in this role, the very manifestation of God's Nature to the earth (for "God IS *love*," I John 4:8) that we must understand the importance of restoring relationships in our lives!

If God IS *love* and He made us FOR love in order to carry it to others, the question becomes, how much of His *love* are we able to receive? I cannot **give away what I don't have** and I cannot carry to others what I have never received for myself.

This is where the problem lies. This is what we have experienced across most of our relationships. We so often find ourselves in a relationship that is like *two ticks and no dog*. Two *needy* people sucking the life out of each other trying to find love is a pretty sorry excuse for a relationship!

When two people come to a relationship looking for love from the other but neither of the two has a reservoir of love from which to give, the outcome is as predictable as it is sad.

We will have to go back to the foundation and uncover those things that have interrupted the flow of God's love into our lives. If we are ever to realize this dimension of *abundant life*, we will have to revisit the places where our intimacy with the *source* was disrupted.

This part of the journey will take patience, but, with determination, we can be restored in our relationships through the healing of our broken hearts. We will need to ask some powerful questions about our relationship with God. What is my relationship like with Father, God? How do I see Him?

What about Jesus, the Son? Have I been able to have *fellowship* with Him so that His love-nature is able to permeate my being.

What about the Holy Spirit? Have I been *teachable* when the Holy Spirit nudges me to change? Am I willing to be *comforted* and *healed* in my soul by the Holy Spirit?

These are important questions that will impact the restoration of our relationships through God's love. Without the full-flow of God's love working through all the dimensions of the Godhead, I will not have the foundation or the fullness of love that I need for healthy relationships.

If I try to jump out there to *rebuild* my human relationships without a complete work in my relationship with God, I will soon find that my *human* love runs dry. By human commitment and determination, I may be able to succeed for a while. But soon my affections will fail because I'm unable to draw from the *love-source* I was designed to receive from ... God, Himself.

Survival, Defense Mechanisms, Habits and Patterns

Even when we have our relationship with God restored and our *love-source* flowing, we may find that residual effects from our childhood still give us trouble. In our fight for *survival*, we may have picked up stubborn habits and patterns as part of our childhood experience.

Many of these patterns are the result of defense mechanisms we've developed. We may even have an array of *survival techniques* that have become entrenched as a response to traumatic experiences.

For one person, the difficulty could be manifest in a defensive anger. They may even display violent rage because they once learned that rage can cause a threatening person to back off. Another person could have an automatic reaction that throws them into the *victim* role because they found that doing this could evoke compassion in others.

These are just a few examples of the many behaviors adults may exhibit during times of stress or when they feel threatened. On the surface, these behaviors may not seem that bad. But, when one of these defense mechanisms becomes so engrained that the reaction is involuntary, relationships will suffer because reality becomes distorted.

If my response to perceived danger is to *trust no one*, it may, in the moment, seem like a reasonable reaction to a threat. But, when this response becomes *hard-wired* into my brain because of trauma and I am completely unable to control it, my relationships are hurt because my habitual distrust is unjustified.

No one sets out to endure the long-term heartbreak of a relationship filled with compulsions and out-of-control behaviors. These hard-wired responses make relationships difficult for both family and friends because most people expect us to regulate our behaviors appropriately.

The truth be told ... most of us have suffered things that have produced habits or patterns in our lives that are difficult to change or control. For those of us who have gone through addiction, you can be almost certain that our relationships have been challenged by defensive behavior patterns left from our childhood. Whether experienced in childhood or self-imposed through our own risk-taking behaviors later in life, traumas have likely left their damaging mark on our relationships and social skills.

Healing Old Relationships God's Way

The truth is that not every broken relationship can be mended and some of them probably shouldn't be. While that is NOT to imply that God is not able to mend any relationship, it is important to note that not all relationships began through the will of God.

One of the most important first steps toward *making room for others* is to do some *sorting* of the relationships I've had. I may need to decide which of my existing relationships are really worth keeping. An honest assessment of the relationships I've developed during *addiction **and** in recovery* may lead me to let go of most of them.

But an important thing to remember when we're asking God's help to restore old relationships is to keep the focus on *me*. No one can really contribute to the mending of a personal relationship by trying to work on the other person. It just can't be done. *Their change* will have to be by their own effort with God and my process of change will have to come through mine.

By keeping the focus on myself, I'll be able to make full use of the authority God gave me to bring about my own change. God did not give me authority to make changes in another person. I may intercede for their protection. I may pray for the grace they need to receive from God, but I do not have the authority to *choose* anything for them.

When my energies are focused on working with what God gave me to work with (myself), I can make steady progress toward becoming the best *me* that I can be. I will have to trust God with what the other person does with what God gave them to work with.

Healing of old relationships can only happen when I give myself completely to God's will and healing process. If the other person does not meet me halfway in their own healing process, I will need to leave them in the hands of God. Nothing will disrupt the work of God in a relationship more than trying to *control* the outcome of His work in another person.

Getting to the Roots To Have New Growth

Sometimes, the hardest part of developing relationships is when we know we have to mature to make room for someone new. *A Life Worth Living Sober* is not lived alongside mediocre relationships that just happened to fall into our lap! No ... the relationships that are part of God's *abundant life* will tend to challenge us to rise higher!

Abundant life only comes to those who are willing to resist the temptation to *settle* for less than God's BEST ... every step of the way. It will mean that I have to get my *fight* back and see my passion for life restored. *Abundant Life* requires *breakthrough*, *deliverance* and the *tearing down of strongholds* (II Corinthians 10:4) to see the outcome of God's LIFE working in me unhindered.

God has raised up many ministers and teachers today that are gifted with wisdom and insight about how to walk us through *inner-healing* and *restoration*. It will be my job to seek them out, to receive, and to resist the enemy until the strongholds are broken, the roots are cut out, and my healing is complete.

Sometimes, when my ego is large and my selfishness runs deep, I may have to experience a dying to the selfish and lazy idolatry I have made of myself. *Making room for others* can be difficult if we have indulged in a *self-love* so big there's no room for anyone else. Letting God's love in first will be essential if we are to truly learn what love is.

A *Life Worth Living Sober* was never meant to be lived alone. Created in the image of God, mankind was designed to be instinctively *social*, *relational* and *interdependent* on others. Just as God, Himself presents the perfection of His being through the *divine family* of Father, Son and Holy Spirit, our experience of *abundant life* is bound up in our success in relationships.

Abundant Life, Because of Love, Because He Promised!

For God so LOVED that He GAVE ... and we will have to learn to *love* and become *givers* too if we are to be like Him. The only way this giving spirit so like the nature of God can GROW is to give ourselves to love and relationships. To *make room for others* is growth itself because it is in *giving* to others that we are automatically stretched to be greater than we were.

When addiction has taken away our capacity to love and has turned us into *takers*, we become so far removed from *abundant life* that it makes it hard to even imagine what it could be like. But Jesus said we could have it. He said, in fact, that the very reason He came was that we *should have* His quality of life and have it more ABUNDANTLY (John 10:10).

Each of us has a choice. I can choose to believe that *abundant life* (including restored *relationships*) can be mine or not. But, if I choose to believe what He said, that He came to give that *life* to me, personally; I will need to grab hold of it as His PROMISE and not let go!

This won't be easy and there will be days that I have to fight for it. But just how much is a life filled with *abundance* really worth? If Jesus thought it was worth laying down His life for, it must really be something worth fighting for!

He came to make me completely WHOLE in every way. He came to help me *get a life* and share it with others in an atmosphere of love and understanding.

"Jesus said ... Get a Life!"
"I have come that they may have life, and that they may have it more abundantly."
(John 10:10)

CHAPTER 10

Transformation

Finding a Life Worth Living

"... I have come that they may have LIFE, and that they may have it more ABUNDANTLY." (John 10:10)

If the Motivation Is Real, We CAN Win the Battle

In the battle for *recovery*, one look in the mirror may reveal something that looks far removed from *abundance*. It may look more like death than it does any kind of *life*. For the addict, even a move in the direction of *abundant life* means only one thing ... *Having a LIFE Worth Living SOBER*!

Those who have fought long and hard can attest to the fact that rebuilding a life from the ravages of addiction is a lot harder than it looks. It seems that God, in His great love and mercy, gives us great faith at the beginning of our journey because that's what we need to get sober. But anyone who's been on the road very long can tell you that *getting clean* and *staying clean* are two radically different things.

Staying clean requires a combination of multiple, powerful motivations. First, we have to settle it in our hearts that God is real and that He truly loves us. We have to believe that His *grace* and *divine enablement* are ever present in our lives to change things.

Then, as we dare to take new risks and try new things, we have to capture an inner vision of new life for ourselves. We have to want it. We have to believe that it's possible to move from our small, self-centered life to a life of fullness and shared abundance with God and others.

It will be scary, and like a toddler learning to walk, we will often fall down. The sharing won't come easy and learning to trust will frighten us like the downhill plunge of a roller coaster. But it will be worth it. No one is ever going to secure this new life for us. There are no shortcuts and there never has been a silver bullet for slaying those demons that still sometimes keep us up at night.

But, if we dare to stand up and ask God for strength to get our *fight* back, we can learn how to SPEAK to the darkness and see it flee from before us. Then, like a warrior who just discovered what he or she is capable of, we will know the Spirit of God fighting though us and we will be able to take back everything the devil has stolen.

THIS is Restoration, a breakthrough out of the revelation that being *born again* is so much more than skipping hell and going to heaven. It is a vision of *life* the way God always intended it to be. I can have that *life* if I understand that I was *born again* for a PURPOSE. If I can believe the *truth* that God is already about the business of rebuilding my life from the ruins, it will become sealed and settled in heaven and no devil in hell can set aside what God intends to do!

The "New Self" Brings Abundant Life

Rebuilding a *drug-destroyed* life is never easy and it's not the struggles with bad habits or battles with fleshly desires that normally give us the most trouble. Because of the damage we've done and the consequences of wrecked relationships, our greatest grief is often caused by the lingering reputation we have earned for ourselves. Trust can be hard to come by and even when we are finally ready to take a *risk* and try something new, it may be hard to find anyone who is willing to take a risk on us!

Family members may not even want us to come by, and when we do, we may see them locking doors or cabinets in the house to keep us from stealing. Something as simple as having a good *reference* for a job may be an impossible task. We may end up sitting alone in a room, staring at the walls feeling overwhelmed by one of those *damned if you do, damned if you don't* moments in time.

But, in that moment, if we will let it, the pressures that have brought us to the brink of giving up and losing our sanity can become the pivot point of our salvation. In that place of *dying inside* there is the unique possibility of rebirth because that is exactly the place where the Spirit of Christ wants to meet us to begin transformation. The *dying* is necessary for REBIRTH.

If we will let the *dying* take place in the atmosphere of His tender *love and care*, His transformation will begin to take place. The bible says in II Corinthians 5:17, *"Therefore, if anyone is in Christ, he is a new creation; old things have passed away; behold, all things have become new." Abundant life* is a *new thing* that God alone can do as part of the new birth in us when we are *born again* by His Spirit.

This experience creates the possibility of a fresh start and a clean slate in a way that nothing else can. It is God declaring us *not guilty* because we are simply no longer that old person who did those old things. *In Christ*, we can become like a *new born baby* that simply has NO PAST and therefore cannot be condemned.

Ephesians 4:22-24 says, *"... put off your old self ... to be made new in the attitude of your minds; and to put on the new self, created to be like God ..."* While it may seem impossible to *change* our old ways and the prospect of others seeing us as someone *new* may seem like a pipe dream, this promise of a spiritual transformation in Christ is REAL.

New Life Always Requires a Little Death and a Lot of SURRENDER

One of the powerful biblical lessons that transformed my life during God's rebuilding process was the truth that God is able to give me a *new nature*. I remember praying one day when I got blatantly honest with God. I told Him that if He didn't do something to change me on the inside ... if He didn't take away those addictive desires and give me new ones, I was never going to make it. I went on to tell God that if He didn't give me a *new life* with *new friends*, that wasn't going to work either! *(I found that God actually loves it when we get honest like that.)*

Soon after that prayer, The Holy Spirit began to take me to verses like, *"(He has given us) ... great and precious promises, that through these you may be partakers of **the divine nature** ... "* (II Peter 1:4) And, *"... be transformed by the **renewing of your mind** ..."* (Romans 12:2). As I meditated on these promises from God, I soon found that I had faith and hope beginning to take root in my heart. It was a transforming kind of faith and I started to believe He could change things!

I soon began to realize that the *new life* and the *new self* that the Bible talked about was something that would emerge from the inside of me. This new hope became a well-spring of life that couldn't be stopped because I decided I wanted it and surrendered myself to it.

It didn't take long for me to discover that the *abundant life* that Jesus talked about was a description of the *quality* of life He brings. What I began to experience was life that makes itself known to its surroundings... through me! This was life, pure and simple, and was immediately known by everyone around me because it was so opposite from the death that had been my life before.

The Temptation To Settle for Less

There was a time in Jesus' life that He had to refuse the temptation to *settle for less*. In the same way, our fulfillment in *abundant life* will depend on how much we learn to live by faith. Satan personally met Jesus in a wilderness place to tempt him to *settle* for a shortcut to kingdom authority. How much more will the one who hated Jesus look at us with eyes of hatred and try to tempt us to settle for less as well.

His coming of age was marked by things that were different from His peers. Mary, the mother of Jesus could surely sense that His destiny was about to come forth because the very atmosphere was pregnant with purpose. There was an anticipation and a knowledge that The Father was watching over His Only Son to ensure that all was as it should be.

The Bible says that "Jesus came from Galilee to John at the Jordan to be baptized..." (Matthew

3:13). Though John at first tried to resist the request, Jesus won over his cousin, John saying it would be a fitting and righteous thing to do. It must have been both confusing and contradictory for John since he saw himself as a forerunner of this One whose sandal strap he was not worthy to loose (Luke 3:16).

In Luke 3:21-22, the Bible says that Jesus persuaded John and that He was Baptized. Suddenly, as if a great Key had been turned in a lock, a powerful transition took place before their eyes. The heavens were opened, the Holy Spirit descended, and a Voice came from heaven saying, "You are My beloved Son; in You I am well pleased."

He was no longer the son of Mary, the son of a carpenter who came from Nazareth. He was now clearly The Son of God, the Heir to The Heavenly Throne!

Jesus was now the King who was also a Priest "according to the order of Melchizedek," (Hebrews 5:10) and His Kingdom was being violently injected into hostile territory (earth). In Luke 4:23, the Bible tells us that "Jesus... began His ministry at about thirty years of age" immediately after His baptism took place.

This event changed Him so much that in Luke 4:1-2, we are told that "Jesus, ... filled with the Holy Spirit, ... was led by the Spirit into the wilderness, being tempted for forty days by the devil." This declaration of Sonship and the coming out of His inevitable Kingship had stirred up a war. The revelation of who Jesus was summoned up the prince of darkness with a kind of vitriol the earth had likely not seen since the days of Noah.

But the serpent was not there to kill Jesus because he wanted to satisfy his curiosity about one thing. He first wanted to find out if it might be possible to own Him. Satan had to test Him to see what authority He had because he knew that legally Man had given authority over the earth to him. The devil wanted to tempt and torment Him and try Him with the authority of the Word to see if this could truly be The King.

Even though Satan joined the battle with Jesus using temptations about stones and bread and taunting questions about His identity, these were never related to the true prize he was after. His goal was simple. He wanted to see Jesus COMPROMISE His calling by choosing a path that would subvert His destiny!

The entire story reaches its climax in Luke, chapter 4, verse 5: "Then the devil, taking Him up on a high mountain, showed Him all the kingdoms of the world in a moment of time. And the devil said to Him, 'All this authority I will give You, and their glory; for this has been delivered to me, and I give it to whomever I wish. Therefore, if You will worship before me, all will be Yours.'"

Never in the history of mankind was there a greater temptation for a man to take a short cut. We cannot fathom what images and thoughts may have gone through the Lord's mind. He knew when He looked at His destiny that He saw unimaginable suffering, a cross, and betrayal by the very people He came to save.

Jesus the man, the human being, stood there pondering how hard His path would be if He stayed with the plan of His Father. He could have chosen what seemed an easier way to become the King and ruler of earth. Instead, He made a choice that sustained Him all the way through even the darkest hours leading to the Cross. "Get behind Me, Satan!," Jesus said, "For it is written, 'You shall worship the Lord your God, and Him only you shall serve'"(Luke 4:8).

Nothing Short of Complete Transformation Will Do

Just like Adam and Eve in the Garden, endowed with the vast freedom to enjoy all of God's *trees*, we are given broad faculties of *choice* and *free will*. We can choose to pursue a path of Godly purpose or to simply go after something less. What we sometimes forget, however, is that it's the quality of our *heart-change* by God's Spirit that will guide our choices to be either in Him or not.

Nothing short of a personal and spiritual transformation by faith will be able to give us a *life worth living sober*. There are many who say they are *born again* and many who will tell you they are in *recovery*. But, there are few, in fact, who find their way to what Jesus meant when he challenged us to settle for nothing less than *abundant life*. Living a *sober* life is just not the same thing as living a transformed, *abundant life*.

In Mark, chapter 4, we read a series of parables told by Jesus that are intended to illustrate the Kingdom of God. Then, in the context of this Kingdom, we are told that Jesus asked His disciples to get into a boat to cross over to the other side. The Bible tells us that "*a great windstorm arose, and the waves beat into the boat ...*" so that the boat was filling with water. When they managed to wake up the *sleeping* Jesus in the back of the boat, the Bible says that "*... He arose and rebuked the wind, and said to the sea, 'Peace, be still!'*"

Most of us will know that the story goes on to say that *"... the wind ceased and there was a great calm. But He said to them, 'Why are you so fearful? How is it that you have no faith?'"* So, Jesus rebuked the wind and the sea and we, just like those disciples, may find ourselves in a *storm* crying out to Jesus to *do something*. But, just like he said to them, Jesus is saying to us, *"why don't you exercise 'faith' and rebuke that storm yourselves?"*

From "Clarity" To Divine Order

The road to *abundant life* is filled with challenges and we face a very real enemy that is committed to keeping us from our inheritance. But IT WILL BE WORTH IT! No one said that the journey to a *life worth living sober* would be easy.

John 10:10 says, *"... that they **May** have Life, and that they **May** have it more ABUNDANTLY."* It doesn't say SHALL have life abundantly! God makes a WAY. But the choice is always ours and we must fight the battles with the grace and weapons God provides.

We may start our journey of recovery and restoration with just a *moment of clarity*, but God intends to take us from there through a transformation that will bring lifelong *vision, divine order,* and *growing faith*.

One of the key elements of a growing faith is something called *expectation*, discussed at length in chapter 3. This kind of expectation can be a powerful cure for our negativity, the *poor-poor-me's*, and the *have-nots*. If we are ever to break out of the cynical and selfish attitudes that dominate our life in addiction, we will have to experience more than a *glimpse* of God's Kingdom. We will need a deep encounter with the hope and divine order that is *normal* to the Kingdom of God.

To move constantly forward into this abundant life, we will need to forge a time-tested strength as part of our IDENTITY in Him. The King's *love* and the King's *courage* will have to course through our veins and become our very own. We will have to get to know this new nature and this new identity better than we knew the old one. We cannot afford to have the devil understand who we are *In Christ* better than we know it ourselves!

The Flow of God's Spirit Creates Peace and Harmony

Powerful connectedness and the total *healing of our relationships* can be ours but only if we complete the course of God's transforming work. And we will know if our alignment is with God and if we are cooperating with His *plan* because the people in our lives will let us know.

The Apostle Paul asks a powerful and revealing question in I Corinthians 3:3 and helps us see the real problem in our relationships this way: *"For where there are envy, strife, and divisions among you, are you not carnal and behaving like mere men?"* He is bluntly telling us that living as *mere human beings* and not as spiritually transformed *children of God* ... we are doomed to relationship failure.

In another place (I Corinthians 2:14), he describes the futility of trying to live as mere men this way, *"But the natural man does not receive the things of the Spirit of God, for they are foolishness to him; nor can he know them, because they are spiritually discerned."* Our acceptance of being a mere *natural man* is ever frustrated by the fact that the mind of man cannot be "renewed" without a surrender to the power of God's Spirit!

It will only be in this place of *surrender* to a Christ-forming, spiritual transformation that we can ever hope to have God's *love, peace,* and *harmony* in our relationships. When we give ourselves to the flow of God's Spirit wholly and completely, He is always faithful to complete His good work within us. Only God can rebuild a foundation of goodness and love toward others in a life that's been ravaged by addiction.

The "BECOMING" Will Tell the Tale

The Bible says in John 1:12, *"But as many as received Him, to them He gave the right to **become** children of God ..."*

One thing to remember is that *abundance* is NOT just something to be measured by an amount or quantity of things. We usually think of *abundance* as meaning having *a lot* of something; but the word actually has a root meaning that signifies something like the *rolling of waves* or an *overflow*. Thinking of the word, *abundance*, as coming from the word, *abound*, we can see that *abundance* is actually an experience of being overwhelmed by something good.

In John 10:10, Jesus was actually saying that He came that we might have (His) *life*, and have it in a way that makes us *overwhelmed* by His *goodness*. The *abundant life* of John 10:10 will become reality and manifest itself in a very personal way to each of God's children. It is not something that can be measured and it cannot be described as merely a great amount of His *blessings*.

Abundant life only comes to those who know the feeling of being *completed* by someone whose absence has always made them feel *empty*. It is a *wholeness* that is clearly known to those who have been rescued from their brokenness. It is the joy of entering a relationship with the only One who can fill that *God-shaped hole* we have always felt inside.

But *abundant life* doesn't stop there. Yes, it begins with a revelation deep in our being and comes with waves of unearthly peace that only heaven could bring, but it brings very practical change as well. A *renewed mind* makes it possible to receive and understand new things about ourselves. Our life of frustration and confusion will begin to pass away and renewed insights about the way God made us will open new doors to fulfillment.

No one can give us a *short-cut* to rebuilding our lives from the ruins of addiction. But the beauty of this Christ-led life of *abundance* is that His Holy Spirit is always there to be our guide. He is our Comforter, sent by the resurrected Jesus to always be by our side and is always working to shine forth from the inside. It is the Holy Spirit that brings forth such a powerful transformation that it gives us a completely new nature!

Will *a life worth living sober* be a perfect life? No, but there is an abundance of *help*, *goodness*, and *joy* that comes with a life-journey led by a loving God. Embracing life with a God-given sense of *purpose* always has a way of making it worth the pain, even in the face of things we don't understand.

This is living LIFE the way God intended it to be. THIS is *abundant life*, and it's what Jesus had in mind when He basically told us to *Get A Life* (John 10:10). He said, "*I came that they might have LIFE... more Abundantly.*" It is how we learn to live life *Positively*, *Connected*, *Courageous*, *Satisfied*, and **Transformed**. THIS is the *life* that rises like a phoenix from the ashes to live *"A **Life** Worth Living Sober."*

"Jesus said, ... Get a Life!"
"I have come that they may have life, and that
they may have it more abundantly."
(John 10:10)

Endnotes

1.   Helen Keller, Let Us Have Faith (Garden City, New York: Doubleday and Company, 1940), 50-51.

2.   Angela Duckworth, Grit: The Power of Passion and Perseverance (New York, NY: Scribner, 2016).

About the Author

Steve and Ruth Fallin have been teachers and administrators in the US and in countries abroad for over 30 years. Their calling as facilitators and organizers in *ministry development* has been utilized in such areas as *ministry training and education, church planting, addiction recovery,* and *family restoration ministries.*

The Fallins are both teachers and writers and have a message of healing for hurting families wherever they go. Steve is used by God in *prophetic ministry* and in *apostolic impartation.* While they are both being used by God in *pastoral counseling ministry,* Ruth is especially called to facilitate *healing* for the brokenhearted who have suffered *family violence* and other *traumas.*

The Bridge is a name that has been associated with the Fallins for a number of years, and, with the publishing of this book, they are launching an independent publishing arm of their ministry called, *The Bridge Publishing.*

You can find out more information on this book and upcoming publications by Steve and Ruth Fallin at: **http://www.stevefallin-author.com.**

Steve and Ruth are currently developing a full-time ministry of *training*, *recovery*, and *family restoration* in Mexico City, Mexico. For more information or to book a speaking engagement, please reach out to them through their ministry website at: **http:// www.restorationhousehub.org.**

Made in the USA
Columbia, SC
19 October 2021

47450952R00091